LORD, HEAL OUR MARRIAGE

PAMELA D. YOUNGBLOOD

Copyright © 2014 Pamela D. Youngblood

All rights reserved. No part of this publication may be reproduced or transmitted in any form or by any electronic or mechanical means including photo copying, recording, or any information storage and retrieval system now known or to be invented, without permission in writing from the publisher or the author.

All Scripture quotations, unless otherwise indicated, are from The King James Version. The KJV is public domain in the United States.

Utmost for His Highest, Oswald Chambers

Interview by Donna Scheibe of the Los Angeles Times with Norman Miller, Pasadena School Psychologist on the subject of feminine dependency.

Illustrations by: Stephanie A. Morgan

ISBN-13:978-1-941733-10-3

Published by EA Books, Inc.
eabooksonline.com

DEDICATION

Lord, Heal Our Marriage is dedicated to John, my beloved of 41 years; to Jess and Lisa, our son and daughter-in-law; to Rachelle and Michael, our daughter and son-in-law; and to Jalyn, Julia, Jana, Jess, Jordan, Vincent, Adeline, John Paul and Evana, our nine grandchildren. Our times together as a family are explosions of life and activity, times John and I will treasure always.

I want to give particular honor and recognition to Mrs. Rita M. Dupuy, my beautiful mother, who went on to be with the Lord on December 19, 2012, at 92 years of age. Mom was fondly called "Maw Maw Rita" by all who knew her. If you were to use one word to describe her, the word *loving* would instantly come to mind.

Angele, a close friend from Chalmette, Louisiana, had this to say about my mother:

"Maw Maw Rita would hold on to your face when she gave you a kiss, and she would always look into your eyes. She could see through to your heart."

My mother was truly a vessel of honor through which the love of God consistently flowed. She saw only the best and believed the best in everyone she met. She was an inspiration and a shining example to every wife and mother in our growing family, setting a very high standard for us to follow. The glow and smile on her face, the love in her heart, and her contagious laughter set her apart. We were extremely blessed to call her our mother.

I want to also honor my dear friend from Picayune, Mississippi, Stephanie A. Morgan, who stepped into glory on March 3, 2012, after courageously fighting cancer. While fighting the good fight of faith, she drafted the illustrations for this book. Stephanie's life was an inspiration. She was a multi-talented person who looked for ways to bless others. If someone had a need she could not meet, she would rally the troops to see that the need was met. She desired to perfect her illustrations, but sickness prevented it. To me, Stephanie's drafts are perfect.

Much appreciation also goes to my pastors, family members and friends for their inspiration to me in writing this book, and to those who helped with editing its pages. Their devoted support and encouragement made this book's completion possible.

CONTENTS

CHAPTER	TITLE	PAGE
Foreword	By Dr. Lisa VanSandt	vii
Preface		ix
Introduction	A Zephyr Experience	xiii
1	A New Beginning	1
2	My Ship Is Sinking!	11
3	A Wife's Purpose	23
4	Your Greatest Investment	29
5	The Agony of Decision	39
6	Arise! Shine!	61
7	A Submitted Life (A Battle on Your Knees)	69
8	Yoked Together For A Purpose	89
9	Ouch! Dying Hurts!	109
10	But, You Don't Know My Husband!	123
11	Harden Not Your Hearts!	131
12	To A Woman Who Has An Ear, Let Her Hear!	141
13	The Tongue Is a Fire!	149
14	A Woman's Influence	157

15	Have You Forgiven?	169
16	Dad, Has the Storm Ended?	183
17	Cried to the Lord!	191
18	A Master Basket Weaver!	199
Epilogue	From The Heart Of Her King *(By John H. Youngblood, Jr.)*	207

FOREWORD

By Dr. Lisa VanSandt, Director
International College of Ministry — Liberty Campus
Arab, Alabama

Lord, Heal Our Marriage says most everything a woman needs to know about being a godly wife. As women and wives, we miss it many, many times. We allow this ungodly world to shape and influence us. Yet, the kingdom of God and the Christian life are upside down and backwards to the ways of this world. When we set our face like flint to become a godly wife, God Himself will use people like Pam Youngblood and her book to set us on the right path. Pam does not just write about being a godly wife; she lives the role. She practices what she preaches. She is a proficient writer, an excellent cook, and a remarkable hostess. She serves her husband well.

Like Pam, I, too, was a woman unyielding to the truth, especially concerning the word "submission." Submitting was *not* easy for me. When I finally understood God's concept in the matter, it became easier—not easy, but easier. God is a God of order; therefore, everything He did at Creation was done in order. He created *all* that mankind would need to survive before He ever created mankind. Order ushers in stability, and it is essential and required to live peaceable lives.

When our roles get out of order, confusion begins to rise. Soon chaos and turmoil move in. We are then constantly battling for headship. Many times, we are unaware of the reasons behind our battles. God has set the man as the head of the family (Ephesians 5:23). It is not merely a suggestion;

it is the order of the family. He has placed the leadership of the family squarely on the shoulders of the husband. He is man enough to handle this responsibility because that is how God created him to be. You cannot push him into his God-given role; you must love him into it. Pam will inspire you with the realization that God can use you, the wife, to encourage, edify and esteem your husband, giving him honor and respect, until he assumes and accepts his leadership role.

As you read this book, you may get mad. Truth somehow makes us angry at times. You may get your feelings hurt, but we cannot live by the way we feel. Pam may even step on your toes a little as she did mine. However, one thing is for sure, *"iron sharpeneth iron . . ."* (Proverbs 27:17a). If you continue to follow her lead, she will lead you into all truth and teach you how to become a more godly woman and wife, living at peace with yourself, with your husband and with your Most High God.

I once heard it said and I repeat it often, "Inside every man is a fool and a king. If you speak to the fool, he will answer. If you speak to the king, he will become that king." I have seen many women bring the "fool" out of their husbands.

I promise you the application of all you will learn in *Lord, Heal Our Marriage* will set you on the right course to living your dream with the king of your castle.

PREFACE

As you may have already guessed, this book contains lessons from the heart of someone with personal experience – *mine*. It is a reflection of my attempts, successes and failures to walk the walk of faith on a daily basis until our marriage was made whole.

These chapters were spawned out of a heart of compassion as I saw marriages falling apart all around me. Seeing divorce increase in the church deeply stirred my heart and propelled me to write these pages. God is for marriage. It is His desire to bring restoration to hurting couples. God remained faithful to lead us through to victory; He will do the same for you.

This book was written over a span of twenty+ years. It was saved on my computer with a hard copy stored in a gift box in my closet for the past several years. So many times, I took it out, read it, tweaked it and wondered how God would use it. I would then put it aside again, telling myself I was not qualified to be a writer. I believed there were others who could do a better or more proficient job. Nevertheless, the Holy Spirit gently nudged me along to pursue getting this book published. Every lesson is based on the truth of God's Word. I have prayed for years over this book. I believe the Lord will touch many lives and marriages through the following pages.

Throughout my years of employment in a church office, I have met many wives who .coveted stronger marital relationships. Unfortunately, many of these wives had no godly example they could follow. Many were perplexed as to what to do or how to begin to generate change in their lives and marriages. Daily circumstances crushed their dreams and served only as regular reminders their marriages were dying. By following ungodly family patterns, they became duplicates of destructive and dysfunctional behavior which led them to seek out their *own* solution--*divorce*--which is not God's solution.

The most challenging times in our marital relationship drove me to seek God who taught me valuable lessons along the way. These lessons were hard to swallow at times. Other times, I angrily questioned God. God's Word is truth, and it is truth that makes us free. Therefore, I felt impressed to share the lessons I learned with wives who passionately desire more fulfilling and intimate marriages. If you are struggling in a difficult marriage and are truly seeking help, be assured this book has been written especially with you in mind.

Wives, my main purpose for writing *Lord, Heal Our Marriage* is precisely this – to pass on to you the same help and comfort God has given me, as instructed in 2 Cor.1:3-4.

> *"Blessed be God, even the Father of our Lord Jesus Christ, the Father of mercies, and the God of all comfort; Who comforteth us in all our tribulation, that we may be able to comfort them which are in any trouble, by the comfort wherewith we ourselves are comforted of God,"* (2 Cor. 1:3-4).

These real-life stories are spotlighted as examples and testimonials to help you better understand certain principles presented from God's Word as they apply to marriage. To prevent confusion, please recognize that events shared from my personal life do not appear in chronological order. These testimonials are only shared to help you, the reader, better relate to the topics covered in this book. I have no doubt you will laugh and cry as you read *Lord, Heal Our Marriage*. One thing is certain. You will definitely learn of God's amazing, unconditional love.

You may struggle daily to make your marriage work, and nothing you try helps. You may live with a controlling, immature, irresponsible or lazy spouse. You may live with a spouse who shows you no love or attention. Maybe your situation seems more difficult. You may deal with pornography, alcoholism, physical or emotional abuse, adultery or drug abuse. Regardless of the level of stress you face in your marriage, *Jesus is your answer.*

When a marriage is in trouble, there is always room for improvement and growth in the lives of *both* spouses. The problems in a marriage are rarely and almost never one-sided. Marriage trouble escalates by responding incorrectly to each other and failing to address the root of the problem.

I can promise you the application of these truths from God's Word will positively affect your home and family. I am confident the Holy Spirit will also begin breathing life into your *dying* marriage. Have no fear. The Lord will not leave you helpless. God's divine plan paves the way for you to be made healthy and whole in every area of your life. Be encouraged. Your marriage is a vital part of God's purpose and plan.

INTRODUCTION
ZEPHYR EXPERIENCE

On Saturday, June 2, 1973, I had no idea what the future would hold for us when I said *"I do"* to an exceptionally handsome young man. I vowed, "For better or worse, in sickness and in health, till death do us part."

I would liken my 41 years of marriage to riding the Zephyr at the now closed Pontchartrain Beach, a fun-filled amusement park. The park once stood on the south shore of the scenic New Orleans lakefront. The Zephyr would climb a track, creeping upward toward the crest of the hill, which stood as a significant landmark high above the park. I remember, as a child, being spooked by the weird and creepy noises coming from the wooden roller coaster. The chains on its cars would grind and click as the Zephyr struggled and strained, slowly trudging upward. It would finally reach the pinnacle, offering a panoramic view. Then, suddenly, with the last car reaching the highest peak and the front car helplessly dangling over the hill, the Zephyr would plunge toward the ground, falling at boundless speed. Focused entirely on their downhill plummet, the riders would quickly lose sight of everything else around them, and nervous stomachs would flip. Approaching bottom brought hope that their ride was soon over. Horror would begin to subside.

To the riders' dismay, their frightening ride had just begun. Immediately following the Zephyr's reckless and speedy descent, there would be another hill to climb to a destination unknown. The sudden and unexpected twists and turns in the track would jerk the alarmed riders back and forth in their cars, whipping them around one curve and then another. There were no seatbelts and no cushions to protect the riders from their bumps and jolts against the sides of the cars. It would take all of the riders' strength to grip the bars. The force of the winding ride was greater than they could control. The terrified riders' shrieks would fill the park, pleading for their ride to stop. The Zephyr would finally come to a screeching halt, thrusting its riders forward. Their relentless ride had swiftly come to an abrupt end. They sat shocked, stunned and relieved. Much to their surprise, they had just survived the most thrilling, exhilarating and spine-tingling ride of their lives. Many of the riders would quickly return to the line for a repeat of their unforgettable thrill.

It may be hard for you to imagine, but our marriage has been an adventure--a thrill ride--much like the Zephyr, with its ups and downs, twists and turns and bumps and jolts.

> *"I had fainted, unless I had believed to see the goodness of the Lord in the land of the living," (Psa. 27:13).*

My husband has been my best friend since age twelve, a boyfriend whom I hoped to marry since age fourteen and my spouse since age twenty. I can honestly say I have loved him almost all my life. We have climbed high mountains filled with exuberance, celebration and spontaneity. We have had low valleys to overcome filled with failure, disappointment and grief. We have also faced startling and unforeseen turns of events which produced fear, clouded our vision and challenged our ability to hang on.

Beyond the mountains, the valleys or the unplanned events that come with living in this sinful, deceitful and complex world, the Lord has managed to do much more than keep us together. He has powerfully saved, healed and restored us, giving us a wonderful life filled with love, excitement and purpose. The joy and blessings of our good times have far outweighed and outnumbered the more difficult ones.

We certainly cannot say we have arrived or we have all the answers. New stages of life present new challenges. We can say, however, Jesus is in full control of our ride. Jesus keeps us safely on the track. He is the main ingredient in our loving and blessed family, and we give Him all the glory.

We have discovered Jesus is the only one who has the power and wisdom to bridge the gap between two independently-minded and uniquely different individuals. All we have to do is trust the Lord with our lives and marriage and enjoy the ride. We cannot allow unfulfilled goals, worry, anxiety, fear or *"if-only-I-tis"* to rob us of the joys of today. As the years pass, we have become more thankful for the reality that every day we spend together as a couple is a precious gift from God. We are not guaranteed tomorrow. No one is.

"God is no respecter of persons," *(Acts 10:34).*

What He has done and continues to do for us, He will also do for you. It is my prayer the Lord will fill your home with such love, joy and peace that everyone who enters it will sense His mighty presence. May your home testify to His greatness!

CHAPTER ONE
A NEW BEGINNING

Do you fear your marriage is failing? Are you tired and weary of working to save it? Have you lost all hope? Are you picking up this book in a desperate search for answers?

I pray you are seeking help. Please realize you are not alone in the feelings you currently possess. The questions repeatedly running through your mind are familiar thoughts to many of us. Is divorce the answer? Would leaving my husband disappoint God? How would my leaving affect our children? Where did I fail? Why doesn't he love me? Why don't I love him? These are only a few of the agonizing questions that plague and frustrate many hurting women today.

Does this scenario sound a little too familiar to you? Your home is full of chaos; your nerves are on edge; you mourn with hurt; you live in fear; and even if you are not at fault, you blame yourself for your marital problems. Your life appears to be in complete shambles with little hope of repair. You feel totally broken. You wonder how things ever reached this point, and it seems you can find no answer. At one time, you were happy. Now, happiness seems like an unreachable dream.

If your storm is sudden or unexpected, you may not feel equipped to handle it. Your pain may seem more than you can bear. Anger and rage may be giving way to grief, and you are thinking nobody cares. If you are fortunate to have someone in your life who is concerned, you may be pushing them away. You may believe they cannot understand or relate to your marital stress. You may feel your situation is hopeless and the only one of its kind. You may fear trusting anyone would be an invasion of your privacy, and embarrassment and pride make you untouchable. You may isolate yourself from all who love you while you attempt to tackle your problems alone. By now, depression and discouragement may be knocking at your door, sucking the very life out of you. You may even be entertaining thoughts of suicide. Listen to me, please. That is *never* the answer!

The agony of decision is a miserable and debilitating condition to be in. Fear and uncertainty arise as ideas bounce around in your head. It is alarming to realize you are not the only one affected by your final decision regarding the future of your marriage. The knowledge your decision will have a snowball effect on your children, grandchildren, parents, grandparents, in-laws, aunts, uncles, friends, church members and every person close to you may seem overwhelming. Your run-away thoughts may imprison you in a pool of emotions and misplaced guilt. Every possibility only serves to add more pain without any permanent solution.

Let me introduce you to your only permanent solution. He is my dearest friend, Jesus Christ. I know you are probably saying, "Oh, please, not religion at a time like this!" No, I'm not offering you religion. Religion in itself is useless and powerless. I'm offering you Jesus Christ who is all powerful. There is a major difference between the two. Religion will put you in bondage. It will not set you free.

There are those who claim true religion, but simply go through the motions. They practice their faith, but they fail to comprehend or identify with the power of Christ's resurrection (Romans 6:5).

> *"Having a form of godliness, but denying the power thereof: from such turn away," (2 Tim. 3:5).*

Believers have something to celebrate. Jesus did not stay in the grave. Death had to bow to His resurrection power. He is alive. Jesus is alive.

Martha, the sister of Lazarus, was just like many of us. When her brother died, she lost all hope. She considered her circumstances and was disappointed and discouraged. She believed Jesus had arrived too late to heal her brother. She gave up and lost faith in Jesus right before her miracle. I'll say that one more time. She lost faith in Jesus right before her miracle. How many times do we give up right before our miracles? Hear what Jesus said to Martha.

> *"Jesus said unto her, I am the resurrection, and the life; he that believeth in me, though he were dead, yet shall he live: And whosoever liveth and believeth in me shall never die. Believest thou this?" (John 11:25-26).*

Let's not be a Martha, believing it is too late for Jesus to respond to our needs or come to our rescue. We cannot allow what we see with our eyes to set or define limits on what God can do in our lives and marriages. Jesus is no longer in the grave. He is not bound by the enemy. He is alive--not dead. He is victorious--not defeated. If we will only believe, the same Spirit that raised Jesus from the dead will breathe new life into us.

> *"But if the Spirit of him that raised up Jesus from the dead dwell in you, he that raised Christ from the dead shall also quicken your mortal bodies by his Spirit that dwelleth in you,"* (Rom. 8:11).

If you listen closely and open your heart to Him, you may hear the voice of Jesus challenging you today. Do you hear Him? Jesus is asking you, "Will you believe?"

> *"Jesus saith unto her, Said I not unto thee, that, if thou wouldest believe, thou shouldest see the glory of God?"* (John 11:40).

He desires we believe and trust Him during our darkest hours and most difficult trials. Jesus proved to Martha He was not too late. He is never too late. At the simple sound of His voice, Lazarus came forth from the grave (John 11:43-44). Once again, death had to bow to His resurrection power.

Even when circumstances looked impossible to man, Jesus was not late. Neither is it too late for God to resurrect your marriage. Jesus challenged Martha by questioning her faith. Is your faith being challenged? Will you believe? When you believe and obey His Words, your life and marriage will spring to life once again. The spirit of death which has been negatively steering and controlling your marital relationship will be dispelled by His mighty resurrection power. You will see and experience firsthand the glory of God as He restores life and actively effects positive change in your lives. You will know what it is to be in the hands of a mighty and powerful God.

Jesus will be a faithful friend to you, one who can always be trusted.

> "…and there is a friend that sticketh closer than a brother," (Prov. 18:24).

He knows what you are going through. He loved you enough to die for you while you were yet a sinner.

> "But God commendeth his love toward us, in that, while we were yet sinners, Christ died for us," (Rom. 5:8).

He is one who understands all your hurts and weaknesses.

> "For we have not an high priest which cannot be touched with the feeling of our infirmities; but was in all points tempted like as we are, yet without sin," (Heb. 4:15).

He is a friend you can trust with every private thought and need in your life. You may be at your very lowest, sinking in grief and despair. Even so, as you bring your needs to the Lord in prayer, He will meet you where you are. He is faithful.

> "O taste and see that the Lord is good: blessed is the man that trusteth in him," (Psa. 34:8).

He loves you, cares for you and is reaching out to you.

> "Casting all your care upon him; for he careth for you," (1 Pet. 5:7).

Will you give your cares to Jesus today? Jesus will accompany you through every storm of life; He will help you through your raging winds.

> "So that we may boldly say, The Lord is my helper, and I will not fear what man shall do unto me," (Heb. 13:6).

Isn't it comforting to know you do not have to walk alone?

> *"...for he hath said, I will never leave thee, nor forsake thee," (Heb. 13:5).*

Jesus is your helper, and you do not need to walk in fear.

> *"For God hath not given us the spirit of fear, but of power, and of love, and of a sound mind," (2 Tim. 1:7).*

Maybe your spirit is broken, crushed like powder and bruised. It is Jesus who understands the hurt you feel. He feels the same pain that is ripping you apart and tearing at your soul. He sees every tear running down your face. He feels the same rejection, discouragement and broken heart.

> *"The righteous cry, and the Lord heareth; and delivereth them out of all their troubles. The Lord is nigh unto them that are of a broken heart; and saveth such as be of a contrite spirit. Many are the afflictions of the righteous: but the Lord delivereth him out of them all," (Psa. 34:17-19).*

He created you and nobody knows you better than Jesus. He also knows your desire for a happy, secure marriage and for a good, faithful husband. He knows how much you want and need a husband who loves you, one you can lean on and trust in and one who is kind, understanding and caring. Jesus knows everything about you. He knows you better than you know yourself--even the most intimate issues of your heart. He knows exactly what you need in a husband, down to the minutest detail. He is concerned with all your needs including your need for a strong, loving and healthy marriage.

In your eyes, your problems may have grown into a gargantuan mountain. Your mountain may seem overpowering and impossible to climb. Perhaps you have lived in a thorny condition for several years and have been struggling to climb that mountain interminably. You may feel you have no strength left to take one more step up that mountain. If you stumble, Jesus will be there to pick you up and carry you. With Him, you will succeed. You will be victorious.

Jesus gives you the power to be a mountain mover. As a child of God, Jesus gives you everything you need to succeed. He is your help in trouble. A *mountain* in your life represents anything that stands in your way and keeps you from fulfilling God's plan and purpose for your life. In the name and authority of Jesus Christ, you will learn to "...*say unto this mountain, Be thou removed, and be thou cast into the sea*" and "*it shall be done*," (Matt. 21:21).

This book is intended for married women who desire a better marriage, especially those who are struggling in troubled and unhappy marriages. Some of you have already committed your lives to Jesus Christ, while some of you have never met Him. I am pleading with you to do one thing before reading any further. Please invite Jesus Christ into your life right now wherever you are, whether it's the first time or the 100th time. Ask Him to forgive you, to give you a new beginning and to cleanse you from all your sins. He will. It is that simple to receive a new life--your new beginning.

You may quietly, but defensively, argue that I do not understand your situation saying:

"*My husband is my problem!*"

"*My failing marriage is not my fault!*"

"*You just don't understand who I am living with!*"

I will not dispute the fact your husband may have issues which have contributed to or caused your marital stress. However, all of us must face one truth, "...*all have sinned and come short of the glory of God," (Rom. 3:23).* We must be willing to accept that *all* includes us.

> *"If we confess our sins, he is faithful and just to forgive us our sins, and to cleanse us from all unrighteousness," (1 John 1:9).*

Each of us must come to Jesus Christ, believe on Him and repent of our sins.

<u>REPENT</u> *– TO TURN AWAY FROM SIN AND TURN TOWARD GOD; TO TURN YOUR BACK ON SIN AND SET YOUR NEW COURSE TOWARD GOD.*

> *"Then Peter said unto them, Repent, and be baptized every one of you in the name of Jesus Christ for the remission of sins, and ye shall receive the gift of the Holy Ghost. For the promise is unto you, and to your children, and to all that are afar off, even as many as the Lord our God shall call," (Acts 2:38).*

Jesus gives us a brand new start. Our sins are blotted out as if they never happened (Acts 3:19).

If you have been deeply hurt, you may have a difficult time surrendering to Christ. In your pain, you may be falsely blaming God for your heartbreak. Let me encourage you. This is the time to turn to Jesus, not away from Him.

Today, right now, begins the rest of your life. Your eternal destiny rests on one choice, whether you will accept or reject Jesus Christ. In an effort to make your life and marriage whole, I am certain you have already exhausted many of your own ideas. All the while, Jesus has been standing by waiting for you to call on Him.

Be courageous and put your hope in Jesus. He will give you the strength you need (Psa. 31:24).

Let's put aside any thoughts and plans to change your husband. By faith, give him to Jesus. Trust the Lord to work in his life. Trust that your husband's heart, regardless of its hardness, can be turned by the Lord (Prov. 21:1).

For now, let's begin with you. Where is *your* heart? Jesus wants to fellowship with you. Why not invite him into your life? He is only waiting for you to call on Him. Jesus promised if we call on Him, He will answer. He will be with us in trouble. He will deliver us and honor us. He will give us long life and show us His salvation (Psa. 91:14-16).

Reach out today and receive God's promise to you. Let's pray.

> *"Heavenly Father, I come to You in the precious name of Your Son, Jesus Christ. I desperately need Your help. I realize that I cannot solve my problems alone, but I am told You are a great and mighty God who loves me and is concerned about me. Please forgive me of my sins and give me a chance to start all over again. Please come into my life and wash me clean. Father, help me each day to be the person You desire me to be, to be a better wife and mother. I want to please You from this day forth. Father, please turn my life around and heal my hurt. Help me to forgive those who have hurt me. I know I cannot do this alone, but I do not want to harbor bitterness in my heart another day. It has only separated me from You. Thank You for hearing me today. Thank You that I can believe in You and trust in You to work in my life, marriage and family. Thank You for loving me, forgiving me and making me a child of God. I love You, Lord. In Jesus' name, I pray. Amen."*

If you prayed this prayer from your heart, welcome to the kingdom of God. You are now my sister in Christ. I am excited for you because I know this is the most important life-changing decision you will ever make. You now have a helper who will never fail you, one who will be with you wherever you go and one who is victor over any obstacle you may face. Hallelujah!

This is your new beginning in every area of your life-- your home, your marriage and your family.

Jesus is now your Savior, Deliverer, Healer and Restorer.

He is your Answer. He is your Help. He is your Lifeline.

CHAPTER TWO
MY SHIP IS SINKING!

Do you worry your ship is sinking? Have you already jumped ship. Do you find yourself in rough, deep waters, desperately swimming for your life?

During times of marital struggles, friends and family want to help by throwing you a life preserver. They offer all kinds of well-meaning advice, encouraging you or discouraging you, building up your faith or tearing it down, ultimately saving you or destroying you. Unfortunately, too often, their counsel is a response to hurt with a desire to offer immediate relief. This can be a mistake.

Good counsel must always be a response to hurt with a desire to proclaim the truth of God's Word.

> *"And ye shall know the truth, and the truth shall make you free," (John 8:32).*

There is nothing wrong with seeking marital counsel. If you need outside help, I would highly recommend it. However, should you require counsel, please choose godly counsel. At a time when you are most vulnerable, you do not want to be led astray. You may ask, "What would you consider wrong or poor counsel?"

Wrong counsel is persuasive words spoken to you about your situation leading you to a decision that directly opposes the Word of God. The Word of God must always be your standard.

Make sure you are receiving solid, foundational truths from His Word which will never lead you astray. His words have been purified and are without dross and shall be preserved forever (Psa. 12:6-7). The Lord will order your steps by His Word. Your steps will be firm and steady, and you will no longer falter (Psa. 119:133).

> *"Blessed is the man that walketh not in the counsel of the ungodly, nor standeth in the way of sinners, nor sitteth in the seat of the scornful. But his delight is in the law of the Lord; and in his law doth he meditate day and night. And he shall be like a tree planted by the rivers of water, that bringeth forth his fruit in his season; his leaf also shall not wither; and whatsoever he doeth shall prosper," (Psa. 1:1-3).*

When you married, you and your husband became *one flesh* (Gen. 2:24). Can you think of any one person closer to him than you are? Not likely. You are the one who has the greatest influence on your husband, and that influence can either be constructive or destructive. Therefore, if you are willing, you are in a key position for the Lord to use you to improve your marriage. In all probability, it will not be your aunt who dearly loves you or a prayer warrior from your

Bible study class who makes a difference. Though, they may both pray for you and give you excellent advice. God has been known to use a variety of approaches and methods to accomplish His purposes in the lives of individuals. He even caused a donkey to talk. Let's not put limitations on whom or what He might use or how He might go about affecting change in our lives.

The sad truth is, loved ones are so close to your delicate situation, it is hard for them to be objective. Often those who love you most cannot bear to see you hurting and will want to spare you from additional pain. They may say--with good reason--the task is impossible and suggest you jump ship. In an attempt to relieve your pain, they may be too quick to tell you what they would do if they were in your shoes.

The fact is they are not in your shoes. As much as they might believe they have the complete and total picture, they don't. They also cannot possibly understand the grace the Lord will give you during your time of need. Only the Lord knows the future; therefore, their heartfelt advice may not always be in line with the will of God for you and your husband.

Our Pastor in Picayune, Mississippi, during one of his Sunday morning sermons, gave one of the best definitions of grace that I have ever heard. It was simply this:

<u>GRACE</u> - THE POWER OF GOD WHICH ENABLES US TO DO THE WILL OF GOD.

The Lord will give you the power you need to accomplish His will. His grace is always sufficient. The Lord will also give you a peace that passes all understanding, a peace you cannot begin to comprehend (Phil. 4:7). His mighty presence in the midst of your storm will give you the strength to stand (Isa. 40:29). It will give you an assurance everything is going to be all right. Give God the reins and let Him be God. Let go and let God. Trusting in the Lord will allow you to soar like an eagle, high above your circumstances. You will not get weary and you will not faint (Isa. 40:31).

A question I sometimes hear is: Should a wife compromise or partner with her husband in shameful or sinful activities in order to keep peace or make her marriage work--such as drugs, drunkenness, pornography, illicit sex, crime or any other belief or activity that would lead her away from her relationship with Christ? Absolutely not! As a wife, your responsibility is always to God *first*, keeping your faith firmly planted in Jesus Christ, and then to your husband *second*.

> *"Order my steps in thy word: and let not any iniquity have dominion over me. Deliver me from the oppression of a man: so will I keep Thy precepts," (Psalms 119:133-134).*

At the same time, if you desire to win your husband to Christ, you must continue to love him. Learn to separate the sin Christ hates from the soul Christ loves. See your husband as Jesus sees him, and love him as Jesus loves him.

Take extra measures so you do not allow yourself to be an igniter of abuse by retaliating with anger, vengeance or an evil tongue. Abuse on both sides can often be avoided if you will allow God to have full control. I have witnessed women coming to marriage counseling screaming, cursing and slapping, etc. Please keep your hands to yourself. Responding to words with physical force will only escalate the situation.

> *"A soft answer turneth away wrath: but grievous words stir up anger," (Prov. 15:1).*

We all realize there are extreme cases where a husband continues to be abusive regardless of how hard a woman tries to prevent it. If you become fearful for yourself or for your children, leave immediately and seek pastoral and/or legal help. Do not submit yourself or your children to danger, ever. Your counselor will most likely advise you to separate at least for a season until safety is restored in your home.

While you are working to save your marriage, be mindful that your walk may be a lonesome one. Your closest family and friends may not understand your decision to continue in your troublesome marriage, especially with the liberal and self-fulfilling views of today's society. Some may think you are foolish or say you are in denial. In an attempt to protect you, some may declare you are making a terrible mistake and will be ready to help you pack your things.

On the flipside, others may be blind to your marriage problems and may not grasp the stress in your marital relationship at all. They may not see the issues going on behind the closed doors of your home. They may think you and your husband have a perfect marriage.

If you have prayed and know the Lord is directing you, your trust must never rest in man's wisdom, but in the power of Almighty God.

> *"That your faith should not stand in the wisdom of men, but in the power of God,"* (1 Cor. 2:5).

Don't worry about the opinions of others. Others will fill your heart with empty words as they tell you what they might do in your situation, advice solely based on feelings. You must also forget your empty words, once spoken in pride, when you truly believed you would never put up with marital conflict. Those words were filled with incorrect views and pre-conceived ideas. It is now time to put aside all pride. Put your total trust in the *power* of your mighty God.

Man's perception of circumstances can be wrong. Years ago, a sweet young married woman came to me at church one Sunday to ask for my forgiveness. For privacy reasons, I will call her Evelyn. I was shocked. I was not aware of a problem with our relationship. She shamefully admitted to me she had been extremely jealous of my marriage. She envied the relationship I had with my husband and coveted gifts he had given me on several occasions. Jealousy continued to build as she watched my husband and I interact. She thought our marriage was perfect and felt hopeless, believing she could never have a marriage like ours. Evelyn confessed she allowed her jealousy to grow into hatred towards me. Isn't that just how the devil works? Jealousy had been eating her alive, and I had no idea she held those ill feelings against me.

Evelyn was listening to the wrong voice and was being deceived by the devil. She did not fully discern our real life and marriage. She also did not recognize the healing God was doing in the two of us. She was blind to the fact our marriage was in restoration mode. There was definitely a time in our past when Evelyn would not have mistaken me for "Princess Pam."

I love this sister dearly! It took real courage for her to come to me and make such a confession. Evelyn's honesty and right spirit set her free. At one time or another, haven't we all been deceived, guilty of believing a lie that the grass was greener in someone else's field? Do any of these sound familiar?

- "I wish my husband was more like Sue's husband. He always opens the door for her."
- "I wish my husband would take me out on dates. Jackie's husband makes Friday night dates a priority."
- "I wish we had a beautiful home like Bob and Linda's. My husband is too tight with money."

- "Paul is such a man of God. Did you hear him pray? I wish my husband was more spiritually-minded."
- "Why can't my husband spend time with me? Angie and Tom do everything together, and Tom likes being with Angie more than golfing with the guys."

Unfortunately, pain coupled with deception can cause us to focus more on obstacles than solutions. Let's stay focused on enriching our marriages!

No one wants the pain and heartache that come with valleys. All of us prefer the thrill and excitement that come with mountaintop victories. Therefore, develop confidence in the Word of God, put your faith in the Lord alone and trust fully in His power. Let's make Psalm 119:127-128 our daily confession.

> *"Therefore I love thy commandments above gold; yea, above fine gold. Therefore I esteem all thy precepts concerning all things to be right; and I hate every false way," (Psa. 119:127-128).*

You must develop an intense dislike for, strongly oppose and recognize the worthlessness of any way that is contrary to the Word of God. The truth of God's Word is and always will be right. Confidence in God's Word goes hand-in-hand with how much you are willing to obey it. The more you experience the blessings of obedience to His Word, the more your trust will grow in Him. If you truly love Him, you will obey His commands (1 John 5:2-3).

God's blessings and favor are <u>conditional</u>.

If you desire to *"eat the good of the land,"* enjoying God's best, you must learn to live in obedience to His Word. His blessings and favor will always follow obedience--never disobedience. In contrast, those who choose to live in disobedience and rebellion *"shall be devoured with the sword."* (Isa. 1:19-20).

By an act of your will, you must choose to bring yourself in line with the Word of God. Will this be easy? Without hesitation, my answer is no. Putting one's self on the back burner is never easy. In fact, you might consider this time as one of the hardest of your life. The reason for this is that yielding one's self to the obedience of Christ means dying to self. The old flesh can no longer have its way. It can no longer have its "rights." If you only have a "trying" mindset, you will fail. I will never forget the day I proclaimed to my sister, "I have rights!" She looked at me and lovingly said, "Rights? No! We really have no rights at all." At the time, this made me very upset and angry. Nevertheless, she was speaking truth. We were bought with a price and are no longer our own. We belong to Jesus.

You must, by a pure act of your will, bring yourself in line with the Word of God. Be determined to settle for nothing less than God's best. Therefore, a war will break out between your flesh and the Spirit of God in you. In other words, your "must dos" and your "feel likes" will be in direct opposition to each other. You will begin to understand the meaning of being *"a living sacrifice"* as you allow the Lord to work through you and have His way in your life. In time, your "feel likes" will yield out of your desire to please the Lord. Jesus will be there all the time, giving you strength and ability to obey His "must dos," as you are *"transformed by the renewing of your mind"* (Rom. 12:1-2).

As you step out in faith, you will learn as I did that the devil will never lead you to do God's will. Neither will your flesh. Therefore, as the following actions apply to saving your marriage, you must train yourself to respond to your feelings and to your fleshly desires by doing the exact opposite. Let us do our husbands good and not evil all the days of our lives (Prov. 31:12).

For example:

- *Instead of anger* – respond with kindness and soft words.
- *Instead of pulling away* – press in like glue.
- *Instead of tearing down* – build up.
- *Instead of leading and controlling* – submit and yield to authority and leadership.
- *Instead of puffing up with pride* – give up your rights and respond with humility.
- *Instead of wanting to be great* – serve.
- *Instead of seeing only the bad* – look for the good.
- *Instead of dullness and boredom* – be cheery, fun-loving and spontaneous.
- *Instead of "iceberg" withdrawal* – be assertively romantic.
- *Instead of unhappiness and hopelessness* – be enthusiastic and full of joy.
- *Instead of speaking words of criticism* – speak words of praise, edification and encouragement.
- *Instead of declaring independence* – show a desire and preference for close companionship.
- *Instead of selfishness* – put yourself last.
- *Instead of being a taker* – give.
- *Instead of harboring bitterness and seeking retaliation* – forgive.
- *Instead of choosing to hate* – choose to love.
- *Instead of fear and anxiety* – trust and believe the best, keeping your faith firmly planted in Jesus.

- *Instead of being ungrateful* – be thankful, having a heart filled with gratitude.

- *Instead of always seeing the negative* – be positive by looking through eyes of faith, believing nothing is impossible with God.

At first, I did not recognize what God was doing in my life. I felt God was more concerned with my husband than with me. Why should I work on being a better wife? I didn't see him trying any harder to be a better husband. I murmured and complained to the Lord. It wasn't fair. I even started feeling very jealous because I didn't see the Lord working on him; yet, He continued working on me. One day, the light finally clicked on, and I grasped what the Holy Spirit had been teaching me in the previous months. He had been leading me to prepare a strong foundation which the Lord could later fill with His love.

Years ago, we learned a motto at our local church which was used in our building program. It stated: "Prepare and the Lord will provide."

I had made a right choice to love my husband, but struggled with past hurts. I had been preparing by applying God's Word to my life and was anxiously awaiting God's provision. You do realize that love is a choice, not a feeling, right? Choose to love, and feelings will follow. As long as I was committing my works unto the Lord, I could trust that my thoughts would be established. Love would follow.

> *"Commit thy works unto the Lord, and thy thoughts shall be established," (Prov. 16:3).*

One Sunday, my husband had been serving as an usher and was standing on the far side of our church. As the service ended, he was busy talking to someone. There was nothing extraordinary about that day that would make it any different from any other. The service had been good, and the presence of God was there. As I reached for my purse and gazed across at my husband, I felt the warmth and power of the Holy Spirit come over me, moving down from my head to my toes. Suddenly, God supernaturally filled me with His love and an amazing love for my husband welled up inside my heart. In one moment, he became the most wonderful man on earth.

Where did that deep love, admiration and respect for him come from? By faith, I had been diligently working to build a foundation God could fill. God was faithful to perform His Word. The Holy Spirit poured love in. Love overflowed to all around me. As you press in with a desire to please the Lord, He will meet you and help you. He will fill your foundation with everything you need to make your marriage strong and healthy.

All you have to do is open the door and Jesus will come in and sup with you (Rev. 3:20). As you submit to God, resist the devil and he will flee. Jesus will draw near to you as you draw close to Him (James 4:7-8). He will not leave you alone to struggle and fall.

Can you picture Jesus taking hold of your hand at this very moment? You no longer have to fight and struggle to stay afloat in deep, treacherous and unpredictable waters. Your rescue boat has come. He will see you through your storm.

LORD, HEAL OUR MARRIAGE

CHAPTER THREE
A WIFE'S PURPOSE

There are several factors that contribute to and result in a healthy and happy marriage. Your marital stress, or at least part of it, may be the direct result of misunderstanding one of those factors. Think about this question before you answer it:

Are you confident you fully comprehend God's purpose for you as a wife?

Unfortunately, many married women have had poor role models or have never been taught from the Word of God. God has designed you with a divine purpose in mind. It is outlined in the first book of the Bible.

"And the Lord God said, It is not good that the man should be alone; I will make him a help meet for him," (Gen. 2:18).

God knows all our wants and needs; and, it is God who supplies them (Phil. 4:19). The Lord has smiled upon your husband and has especially chosen *you* as his helper. You are right, fully adequate and God's perfect choice for him.

God understood man's need for help. For that reason, he created Eve as a companion and a help for Adam. Today's society continually degrades the husband as the leader and priest of his home--which is God's divine order--and elevates the wife as smarter, better and in control. If you don't believe this, watch the commercials on television. The advertisements continually portray women as having all the brains, and men as being irresponsible wimps needing to be led around on a string. Should women treat men like they are inferior, weaker or less intelligent? Should women battle for control over their husbands? Most definitely, not.

Yet, we do not have to look very far to see homes being led by women. I was in Schwegmann's Supermarket one day and saw a wife physically and verbally attack her husband. She cursed him and beat him in the head with a loaf of bread, simply because he picked up the wrong brand, a brand she did not like.

Are there still homes where men are respected? In today's homes, we see more men staying home to take care of young children. In businesses, we see more women supervisors and more women applying themselves to qualify for executive positions. In churches, we see more women teachers and leaders who have applied themselves to the Word of God and prayer. There's not one thing wrong with men giving time to their children, with women being promoted to supervision or with women being used in church leadership. Please don't misinterpret what I am saying.

The fact is that God created men to take the leadership role. Where are the men? God wants men to lead. God wants men to take responsibility. God wants men to take their position of authority. That is God's purpose for them!

A wife usurping authority over her husband is wrong. God's Word does not teach this at all. This behavior is the result of wrong thinking polluting today's families. Do not be misled and in rebellion, or through wounded hearts, view men as incompetent fools. To the contrary, God created men, calls men and desires men to be leaders. As a wife, you are chosen by God to be your husband's helpmate. That is your purpose!

> *<u>HELPMATE</u> – A HELP SUITABLE TO HER HUSBAND MORALLY, INTELLECTUALLY, SPIRITUALLY AND PHYSICALLY AS HIS COUNTERPART.*

It took many years for my husband to become the leader God called him to be in our home. Like many wives, I had a microwave mentality, wanting change to occur immediately. What I wanted did not happen overnight. Praise God! It did happen.

We must learn to wait on God. The Lord patiently and steadily worked with my husband, training him, encouraging him and raising him up to be a strong leader. In God's timing, he took on the role of God-given leadership. Throughout the last several years, he has filled a wide variety of very high-level leadership positions. How did this happen? It was God who called him to leadership, and it was God who prepared and qualified him. God used all types of situations to train him, situations that did not involve me. Surprised?

All of us realize a good athletic team cannot function well with all coaches and no players. Every position is necessary and equally important. There are no exceptions. On a professional baseball team like the Orioles [my grandson's favorite team], what contribution would the pitcher be to the team if he refused to pitch and he demanded to play center field instead? The talented center fielder would be robbed of accomplishing his best and fulfilling his purpose on the team. The rebellious pitcher, unwilling to pitch for the overall success of the team, would also cripple the entire team and destroy its ability to win the game. Professional players are hired and trained to fill particular positions on the field; they do not rebel by telling their coaches they refuse to fill those positions. Yet, we see men and women every day who rebel against their Head Coach by refusing to fill their God-given roles, the roles He created them to fill.

The Lord created you and your husband as a team. The idea of two becoming one is a great mystery. Don't you think God is showing us one cannot be 100 percent complete or whole without the other? Husbands will be held accountable for the leadership of their homes. Wives are called to come to their aid, offering help, support and assistance. Husbands and wives need each other. Both positions must be adequately filled and working together in order for the couple to fulfill God's purpose.

When my grandson was just beginning to play Blast ball, an introductory game to T-ball for young tykes, he swung the bat and hit the ball directly toward the pitcher's mound. In his excitement, he immediately ran out in the field after the ball rather than running to first base. Even though he had not yet perfected his role, this energetic four year-old was filled with enthusiasm to learn the game.

There are husbands today who do not understand their God-given role. Many men are set in their ways and lack a desire to learn. Many refuse to change or improve. As a result, they are causing confusion in their homes. They fail to understand God's divine role for them as leader and priest. As a result, frustrated wives are stepping up and taking the lead.

There were times I mistakenly tried to lead our family, but I found this was clearly not God's plan. In the absence of strong leadership, it becomes a little too easy for a wife to slip into the leadership role. Don't fall into this trap. Your husband's leadership is like an umbrella of protection sheltering your marriage. Both roles are equally important to God. The Lord created you as a unique individual and filled you with abilities, talents, dreams, goals and potential. God knew exactly who you were when He gave you to your husband as a gift to him (Prov. 18:22; Prov. 19:14).

Your God-made union is complete when your husband fills his role as the priest and leader of his home and you fill your role as his helpmate.

You are to follow him as he follows Christ. This is the ideal. Sometimes, you must reconcile the real with the ideal. In doing so, always guard and protect your relationship with Christ. Your husband's leadership should lead you to a more intimate personal relationship with Jesus Christ. His leadership should *never* lead you away from Him.

Stay firmly planted in Jesus, the author and finisher of your faith.

LORD, HEAL OUR MARRIAGE

CHAPTER FOUR
YOUR GREATEST INVESTMENT

Have others ever mistakenly thought you had a perfect marital relationship? In fact, have they ever added additional pressure to your struggling marriage, having no idea your marriage was in trouble? They may have asked your husband to teach, coach Little League or lead in some other capacity. They may have asked you to head the PTO, teach Sunday school or entertain in your home. Under normal conditions, you would be happy to oblige every request. However, let me ask you this important question:

"Where are you investing your time?"

With a marriage in trouble, your time is a commodity to be treasured. Use it wisely. As wisdom leads you, there will be times when your best answer to some of these extra-curricular activities will be "no."

What if you were working on a job and eager for a promotion? You would make it a point to look for anything you could do to shine as an excellent employee. You would look ahead, prepare for future projects and anticipate your employer's needs. You would look for ways to get better organized, to make your employer's job easier and to relieve the stress and pressures of the workload. You would be punctual and dedicated. You would work hard. You would put in overtime when necessary. You would do whatever it takes to perform your job with excellence.

What if you desired to be part of a ministry? You would be faithful and assist any way you could. You would be someone your church leadership could depend on, handling your duties with thoroughness and efficiency, while going the extra mile to minister to the needs of those you serve. You know to do your best when it is in the power of your hand to do it (Prov. 3:27). It is a daily practice to put others before you.

Why do you think it is easier to apply this type of "whatever-it-takes" dedication to your job or ministry and difficult to apply this same dedication to your marriage and the husband you love? Are you giving the most only where you are praised and appreciated the most? Are you taking your marriage and husband for granted?

In those outside roles, you may have received compliments, raises or gifts, all saying "thank you" for a job well done. You feel a sense of accomplishment and affirmation at the job. At home, does your husband notice how much you are trying to please him? Does he praise you for the things you do? Even after a full day of juggling children, cleaning, cooking, errands, along with a full-time job, does his face display a disappointing look as soon as he walks through the door, indicating he was expecting more out of you? At these times, the enemy begins whispering in your ear. Are you wasting your time? Are you feeling unappreciated? *Beware.* It will not take long before you quit trying and your efforts are redirected to hobbies, friends, jobs or other self-fulfilling desires. Unfortunately, your marriage eventually loses its rightful place on your list of priorities.

Your focus cannot be redirected by feelings. Your sense of accomplishment in the home must be fulfilled by the assurance you are obeying and pleasing Jesus Christ, even when no one in the family notices or appreciates your efforts. Emotions should not control you or dictate your actions.

Having a job or ministry is certainly not a sin and having one does not mean you are acting out of God's will. Are you and your husband in agreement regarding you taking on these additional responsibilities? Ask yourself, "Where does my husband fall on my list of priorities? Does he fully approve of me doing this? Are we in this together?" If the two of you are not in agreement, your time spent elsewhere can quickly create an added burden on your family, one that he is not willing to support.

Let's consider another spoke on this spinning wheel of life. You may come home from a hard day at work mentally and physically exhausted. In your mind, you have earned the right to relax, and you are pleased to finally have a little time for you. Your idea of hurrying home may be to soak in a hot tub, plant some flowers, exercise, read a book or have your husband cook supper or pick up take-out. In other words, you want time for *you*, time to do what you want to do. You think you deserve this time, right?

Some women routinely postpone going home after work. Might *self* be seated on the throne of their hearts?

Maybe. Many working wives make it a habit to go shopping, work out at a gym or visit a friend after work. Honor and respect for their husbands seem to be greatly lacking in their marital relationships. They feel no sense of responsibility to their husbands, and many don't even bother to call home. Would you consider these actions a form of neglect if your husband routinely did not come home to you in the evenings?

Many married women fight and argue with their husbands over time spent with friends. They believe they should have the right to go out with them whenever they please. They still try to hang on tight to their old freedom. This is not a wise choice, especially for wives who are working to *save* their marriages. *Guard* yourself and *use* wisdom, even more so with single or unbelieving friends. The enemy will make sure you see being single as a lifestyle of freedom, happiness and adventure. Many married women see no danger in continuing relationships with their old male friends, even some they previously dated. They will continue to e-mail, text or message on Facebook. These soul ties must be broken. Don't play with fire. Given the right circumstances and pressures of life, the enemy can set you up for a fall. Those old dying embers can reignite into flames of trouble. There is definitely a place for friendships in your lives, but your relationships will need to be redefined as you realign your priorities as a married woman.

Years ago, I prayed with a middle-aged woman (we will call her Susie) who had been married about fifteen years. She initially came to me for counsel regarding a personal tax matter. After a few minutes of conversation, I found out Susie was maintaining a very close relationship with a male family friend. This friend was her confidant. She had shared her most private emotional needs with him. She looked to him for leadership and guidance, and she honored and highly respected this man's counsel. This friend was satisfying emotional needs in Susie's life, ones that should have been met by her husband. I recognized immediately that their marriage was in trouble.

Your choices must line up with your goal for a new and improved Christian marriage. They must line up with the Word of God. If you are sincerely working to better your marriage, you need to be geared up to change hats and place leisurely activities on the back burner. Your day does not end when you arrive home. It has only begun! Your spouse will be looking for you to minister to him. You will have to guard your heart to keep this type of mindset, but your husband should always come first if you are serious about improving your marriage. If you ask the Lord, He will give you both energy and enthusiasm on your most exhausting day.

Think about how you can better care for your husband. Ask yourself: Have I considered him when planning my day? Am I holding off decisions until I receive his input on important issues? Have I touched heaven in prayer for him today? Have I relieved him of pressures and responsibilities so home can be his refuge and place of rest? Where will I be when he arrives home? What might he like for supper? Has he made any plans for us tonight? Would he enjoy a romantic evening? Will he be coming home from work stressed and physically or mentally exhausted? Are things peaceful and orderly at home? Have the children completed their homework? Are the babies bathed and ready for the night? Have I prepared myself for his arrival home?

All of us consider some of these things some of the time. Unfortunately, if we are honest with ourselves, many of us do not routinely give our husbands the consideration they deserve. If you want God's best in your marriage, doing something special for your husband now and then or giving him a little extra effort once in a while will not be enough.

Instead, your tireless, selfless, loving care will be needed every day without expecting anything in return.

It may be a hobby that utilizes your time and has your focus. You are the only one who honestly knows if you are trying to escape reality by running to something you find easier or more enjoyable. Are you dodging your God-given responsibilities? If you are spending too much time or money on hobbies, consider realigning your priorities. Hobbies are time-consuming. Your hobbies don't have to end, but try limiting the amount of time you spend on them.

Everyone knows the demands of being a good mom can be all-consuming. Large families naturally require much of a mom's time and energy, and there is not a whole lot she can do to change that demand. Time can also be a challenge for a mom of an only child because that child has no siblings to keep him occupied, and he looks to his mom for entertainment as well as needs. Mom, before you realize what is happening in your home, is your husband going to bed alone while you are attempting to finish up for the night? Has the entire evening gone by without spending any quality time with your king? Your neglected husband may try hard to be understanding, but he certainly will not feel loved by you if this routine continues night after night. He needs his time with you too. He needs his place of importance in your life. Find time to treat him like a king. Teach your children his place of authority in the home by the respect, admiration and attention you personally give to him. By the example you set, teach your children to honor their Dad and to give him a hero's welcome when he arrives home.

It is perfectly natural for a mother to nurture and care for her children. Because this comes so naturally to a woman, wives mistakenly assume their husbands respond the same way and their children's needs always come first to fathers as well. When a wife responds to her crying baby, for example, she assumes her husband is on the same page. She believes she is taking care of a need that is a first priority to both of them and pleasing him in the process. She may not be aware of her husband's frustration, selfish though it may be, when she is drawn away from him so often. For this reason, wives usually end up surprised with the realization the marital relationship is their top priority--not the children--though they truly love their children.

If you are seriously striving to be a better wife, I strongly recommend you put your own feelings aside and make your marriage top priority. You should take note of where you spend your time. Are you sleeping too late or napping too long? Do you spend hours surfing the web, reading a book, texting, instant messaging your Facebook friends or talking on the phone? Do you find your day flies by and very little is accomplished? Do you spend your day doing whatever you please? Do you spend your day shopping or visiting others? Do you have to rush through the house like a white tornado thirty minutes before your husband's arrival home? Do you wait until the last minute to prepare supper only to realize everything is still frozen? Do you enjoy being with your friends more than being with your husband? Your marriage cannot be all about you or about what makes you happy. Your mindset must change from what pleases *you* to what pleases *your king*.

Stay focused on your goal--working with God to save your troubled marriage.

Is your marriage worth it? You better believe it is; but, you must do things God's way. What can you possibly do to make your husband's life easier? Are you praying for him? What might he appreciate or enjoy? Be creative. How can you lighten his load or relieve his stress? Do you listen when he speaks? Do you anticipate his needs without him having to ask? Do you serve him and prepare his meals? Do you remember to take care of his special requests? How are you ministering to him? Do you keep romance alive in your home with mystery, fun and spontaneity? Do you show him honor and respect? Do you put his needs before your own? Do you set an atmosphere in your home he finds so pleasurable that he looks forward to coming directly after work to his castle and queen? Don't ever believe the lie your efforts will go unnoticed. Be persistent. Your husband's pride may not allow him to respond immediately. In time, he will reciprocate the love and attention given him.

In my dad's later years of employment, he frequently remarked that as soon as he heard the whistle blow in the evening ending his day's work, he would quickly jump into his truck and head home. He teasingly said his truck knew its way home and could get there without him. He didn't want to stop anywhere for anything. There were never any detours. Why? The king couldn't wait to get home to his castle, where his queen was waiting with loving, open arms. He often referred to his home as his castle where all of us treated him like royalty. There was no place in this world he would rather be than home where he was accepted, respected, honored and loved.

As you pray and seek the Lord regarding your marriage, the Holy Spirit will begin showing you your husband's heart. Be responsible for contributing to the overall success of your marriage. This is no time for laziness. Pay attention to him. Attempt to learn more about him--what he likes and does not like--or what thrills him or upsets him. The more you pray for him and with him, the more the Holy Spirit will reveal your husband's heart to you. Prayer produces intimacy. I remember when we first began praying together. I was very surprised to hear how he prayed over certain situations. I quickly discovered I had been guilty of second-guessing his reasoning. Praying together helped me to better learn his heart. Prayer brought us together in one accord.

Some close friends were a great inspiration to us in this area. When praying together, they would hold hands and face each other. When things are not right between a husband and wife, this is very difficult to do. This type of intimate prayer time between husband and wife helps the couple learn each other's hearts, i.e. struggles, fears, worries, anxieties, unbelief, etc. It will also melt the hardest of hearts.

God, who created you to be his helper, will not leave you in the dark. The Holy Spirit will teach you to be an excellent helpmate. Each day, be willing to awaken early and go to work. Learn to be a wife of great value. It is a new day and you have a new job assignment--a job with a great benefit package.

Your ship may have taken a strong hit. It may have collapsed or broken up into a thousand pieces. It may have taken on water causing it to sink. Regardless of how bad things might look to you right now, the Lord sees right where you are and exactly what you need. I promise He will not let you drown. Your rescue boat is waiting. Don't let it pass you by.

LORD, HEAL OUR MARRIAGE

CHAPTER FIVE
THE AGONY OF DECISION

The agony of decision is similar to the game of tug of war, you being the rope which is being pulled and stretched so thin, it is ready to break. I'm sure I can closely relate to the thoughts you are currently entertaining in your minds. At one time, I was not convinced I wanted to commit myself to my marriage either. I felt I had given my marriage more than 100 percent. I was tired and burned out, feeling like I had tried everything and had nothing left to give. I wondered if my marriage was worth the fight. Hindsight says, "Most definitely, yes!"

Today, it is easy to see that Satan has launched an all-out attack against the church. He is doing this by destroying families and homes all over this world. Satan has an agenda to steal, kill and destroy (John 10:10).

Several years ago, I was told by a former cult member in Wiggins, Mississippi, that her cult group had been praying and fasting for the total destruction of families. Not only is it the devil's aim children not be raised by their natural mothers and fathers, it is also his aim they be raised in homes where the meaning of family is distorted and perverted.

Today, school curriculums are being changed to present this perversion to our children as normal family life. Television programs portray perverted family values. We see twisted and reversed parental roles and dysfunctional living conditions in the home which the present generation is accepting as normal family life. Our country's leaders are calling "evil" good and "good" evil and placing this perversion into law.

Satan's attacks are visible in today's society with more divorces than ever before in history, even in the church. More and more couples today are living together, choosing to avoid God's covenant of marriage. Satan's tactics of perversion and deception are evident with the rise of homosexuality and gay marriages, with adoptions by such, totally misrepresenting the Biblical meaning and purpose of marriage where one man and one woman become "one flesh." Why? I believe the devil's days are short, and he knows weak and struggling families make powerless churches.

God sets the standard of what is right and wrong, not man; He clearly states in His Word these things are wrong.

> *"Know ye not that the unrighteous shall not inherit the kingdom of God? Be not deceived; neither fornicators, nor idolaters, nor adulterers, nor effeminate, nor abusers of themselves with mankind,*

Nor thieves, nor covetous, nor drunkards, nor revilers, nor extortioners, shall inherit the kingdom of God," (1 Cor. 6:9-10).

There is also hope extended to those who turn from their wicked ways. Haven't all of us sinned and come short of His glory?

"And such were some of you: but ye are washed, but ye are sanctified, but ye are justified in the name of the Lord Jesus, and by the Spirit of our God," (1 Cor. 6:11).

Before you make a hasty decision regarding your marriage, stop. Please stop. Quit taking matters into your own hands. *Pray.* Determine in your heart to take your need for a better marriage to the Lord. Seek His wisdom. Is any situation impossible for the Lord? I think not.

The following story describes many of today's marriages. I will name this couple Joe and Sally. For years, Joe and Sally's marriage had been slowly deteriorating, making them increasingly unhappy. They lost hope of their marriage improving, growing or ever becoming intimate. They believed they were no longer in love. Yes, Joe and Sally lived under the same roof. They busied themselves with everything possible. Joe worked hard and devoted his time to furthering his career. Sally also held a full-time job while managing their household. Joe and Sally's responsibilities continually pulled them apart until Joe's life became entirely independent of Sally's. They no longer shared any common ground. They no longer shared good, quality time with each other. Joe and Sally became disheartened with their marriage and were ready to throw in the towel. "Let's call it quits," Sally said. This prison of discouragement and mediocrity can lead to loneliness, a deadly snare for any man or woman.

Believe it or not, many couples continue living in this type of self-inflicted prison. They refuse to admit they are living an imitation. Some choose to remain in this phony, lonely, hurtful condition for their children's sake. Others are afraid of losing their financial security. Be honest with yourself. Do you need help with your marriage? Denial will never bring about healing.

John and I fell into a similar trap, living two independent lives. For a long time, we didn't realize it. Our marriage didn't start out that way. Like you, when we first married, time with each other was top priority. The world stopped in order for us to make time for each other. Nothing was more important. Unfortunately, the day-to-day pressures of life and the demands placed on us with jobs, ministries, children, sick parents, etc. pulled us in opposite directions. It was almost as if there was an invisible line drawn down the center of our home where we divided up the responsibilities to make things work. We lived in the conquer mode. Our home was managed very well, but it seemed quality time with each other was so hard to find. Everything and everybody else's needs *always* came before our own.

The fact is you must *guard* your time with your husband. You must make it your priority to have that special time with him. If you don't, the cares of life will quickly eat your time away. Your marriage will miss out on the intimacy that only comes with spending quality time together.

Many years ago, I crossed paths with a dear elderly lady who I will call Denise. Denise was married to Ed. Denise had settled for a marital arrangement through most of her married life. Her acceptance of Ed's sin had become the norm. Each Friday, Denise reluctantly prepared Ed's clothes, packed his suitcase and sent him off to be with his mistress for the weekend, only to receive him back home again

Monday morning. Denise had accepted this arrangement out of fear. She feared spending her later years alone, having no financial security and living without health insurance benefits should she become ill. She depended on Ed to meet those needs. Certainly, this was not God's plan for this couple. Sadly, Denise was deceived into accepting an ungodly arrangement as her way of life. Without a doubt, Denise needed Jesus to intervene in her home. Surprisingly, there are many women living in similar situations who do not know they can reach out to Jesus.

Recently, I came across a situation with a lady I thought to be uncommon, only to later learn it is quite common. I will call this lady Debra. Debra is 100 percent content with her dysfunctional arrangement. She has no idea her marriage is dysfunctional. To Debra, her marriage is perfectly normal. She sees no need to set higher standards for her marriage. Debra and Doug sleep in separate rooms. For the most part, they have very little to do with one another. They rarely talk. They fulfill separate duties in their home. Debra and Doug are both responsible individuals and cover the necessities of running their household. When Doug arrives home, he eats dinner which Debra prepares for him. He then spends the rest of his evening on his computer in his bedroom behind a closed door. Debra believes he is visiting chat rooms. It is difficult for me to fathom how it would feel to live with a man every day and never receive love from him. What a shame. Is this a real marriage? No, it is not. Having no better example of marriage in her life, Debra has readily accepted this marital arrangement as a normal marriage and does not see the need for improvement. Since she has a roof over her head and the bills are paid on time, she has been deceived into believing this is marriage. Why would it need to be better? How many couples might you know who have settled for a similar ungodly imitation of marriage?

Many young couples today refuse to take responsibility for their God-given roles, one spouse putting the entire burden of the marriage on the other. Many wives expect the husbands to handle everything, taking no part in the responsibilities of the home. Many men refuse to provide, causing the wives to mistakenly take the lead and become the bread winners. When these marriages go sour, these couples immediately run to the courts to file for divorce. Part of their problem is they have bought into a dysfunctional view of family life. God's plan for marriage is so much better than this.

So, let me ask you this question:

Will you consider giving God time to restore your marriage?

Your choice must be built on a bond of love called commitment. Though the right choice, it is difficult for many women to choose this option after counting the cost. It will require effort and time. It will require change. It will require trust in God and a removal of the limits we place on Him. It will require forgiveness. It will require humility. It will require prayer. Regrettably, many wives find it easier to give up. What about you? Will you look through eyes of faith and see a caring, mighty and able God?

We cannot fathom how to heal ten, fifteen or twenty years of hurts. Our lives feel so tangled we cannot see where to begin. It is at this point we must let go and let God. He is the Alpha and Omega, the beginning and the end. He already knows how the story ends. He will guide us there if we will set our wills aside and let Him have control of our lives.

Unfortunately, more often than not, we are controlled by our negative circumstances, causing us to lose sight of our goals. Focusing on our own pain or anger only breeds depression and bitterness. We are then less willing to forgive and forget. We are then less adaptable to change and less willing to express love to our difficult husbands. In a nutshell, we are definitely not willing to die to self.

As deception escalates, it leads to divorce. We spend too much time listening to the devil's lies and begin believing we have no other recourse. In general, a greater determination is placed on running and escaping than on resolving marital conflict. What appears to be the easy way out is often a trap, one you can spend the rest of your life in and one which can have a devastating effect on your children, as well as on their children.

Difficulties in a marriage often *shout* some of the following:

- *"I am not a good wife."*
- *"He has never loved me."*
- *"I am a failure."*
- *"I cannot satisfy him."*
- *"It is my fault he is not happy."*
- *"I am not attractive."*
- *"I am boring."*
- *"I must change."*

These thoughts tear down a woman's self-esteem and build a "poor little olé me" mentality. Unfortunately, women have these thoughts and feelings, taking on the guilt, regardless of who was at fault. Even when not at fault, a wife is quick to question what she did wrong. The best way to combat these negative thoughts is to make a declaration of faith:

> *"Lord, with Your help, I will be a godly wife. According to Your Word, I will make what changes are necessary in my own life. I will be a blessing to my husband and not a curse. In Jesus' name."*

The devil will go for the jugular and attack your self-worth, especially if there is infidelity involved. A victim of infidelity most often believes if only she had been prettier, thinner, taller, sexier or endowed with a model figure, her husband would never have strayed. If this is you, don't be deceived. God created all women with unique and varied appearances, personalities and inner qualities. Another woman has nothing on you. God created you with everything you need to make your marriage complete. You are the gift God gave to your husband. Stand up right now and look in the mirror. Tell yourself, I am a marvelous work of God, and *"I am fearfully and wonderfully made"* (Psa. 139:14). Quit believing the devil's lies that you are not enough. Each person makes his own choices. You cannot accept responsibility for another's choice to sin.

It would not be fair to address the men and say nothing of the women who stray from their marriages. Today, the number of extra-marital affairs is almost equal, i.e. husbands cheating on wives and wives cheating on husbands. Even more alarming are the increased numbers of husbands leaving their wives for other men and wives leaving their husbands for other women. Moral values are decreasing at an unbelievable and shocking rate.

At a recent conference I attended, there were as many women as men going to the altar to repent of pornography. It was recently reported by a Pastor friend that sexual experimentation, including girls with girls and boys with boys, is now beginning in junior high grades. Today, the number participating in sexual sins is on the rise.

Whatever the reason for trouble in your marriage, refuse to give the devil one more inch of the land God has given you--your husband, your family and your home. There will definitely come a time in your life when you must take a stand. It is up to you. Be the woman of God who will say,

"Devil, I'm not budging!" When God is on your side, who can stand against you?

> *"What shall we then say to these things? If God be for us, who can be against us?" (Rom. 8:31).*

Realize running is not your answer. Your problems will only follow close behind. Stand up. Face your problems. Overcome them in Jesus' name. The lessons you learn while walking through your trials will deliver you to a stronger and more promising future.

Do you honestly believe the grass will be greener if you leave your husband? Do you really think a relationship with another man at some unknown time in the future will be problem-free? Don't be deceived. Your fantasy man will not be perfect either. It is only God who can effect change in our lives. Pray for God to work in your own husband. He is the man you married, the man you chose and the man you vowed before God to be with *"till death do us part."*

Through the years, many couples came through our church office for marriage counseling. Many were reaching out for solutions. Others had already made up their minds. They were really only hoping to find someone to confirm the choices they had made. There were some who had already divorced and remarried, and now, found themselves struggling once again. Many of these spouses were asked: "If you knew then what you know now, would you have worked harder on your first marriage?" Surprisingly, a large majority said yes.

Some church organizations have amended their wedding vows to read, *"as long as they both shall love"* in order to satisfy the less traditional brides and grooms who are unwilling to make lifelong commitments to each other. Do these couples realize they are entering their marriage covenants anticipating failure and preparing for a way out? Sadly, they are using the church to support their fear of commitment. Let's be honest. There will be days we will not feel "goose-bump" love for our husbands, but this is no reason for divorce.

Stop dwelling on the mistakes that caused your present marital stress. Has your husband failed? Have you failed? Have you been placing false guilt on yourself for your husband's failures? Regardless of who's at fault, all of the worrying in the world cannot change one minute of the past. However, obedience to God's Word and faith in a God who can turn any situation around for your good, will give you a much brighter future. The devil would love to keep you bound in a woe-is-me pity party. Such a pity party wastes valuable time which could be better spent improving your marriage.

How do I know this? I've been there. The ups and downs of my husband's walk with God--excitement and renewed hope with every victory and then hitting rock bottom with every setback--put me on an emotional roller coaster. One day, I was a woman of faith. The next, depression would move in, and I would be as low as a snake's belly. One day, I would be battling pride because things were so great. The next, I would wallow around in self-pity, suffering from a deflated self-righteous, better-than-you mentality. All the while, I continued pointing my finger and defending my disclaimer to having made any contribution to our marriage trouble.

One day, the Lord helped me to see the light, and I realized I was nothing without Him. This was a frightening realization for a woman who was filled with pride and self-confidence, and up to this point in her life, had been an overachiever.

My hard head and refusal to receive instruction from man turned me to God's Word. This particular day, I had searched God's Word to find out what He expected of me as a Christian woman. I found myself in Proverbs 31, studying the qualities and character of a godly woman. I just broke down and cried and asked for His forgiveness. I remember telling Him, "Lord, I cannot be this kind of woman."

Following God was my greatest desire. My actions, though, had been driven in the wrong direction by responding to a myriad of negative circumstances. I should have been responding to the Word of God instead. For example, I had little desire to pamper, serve or care for my husband. I regularly spoke critical words to him rather than words of life. I felt he had taken my love for granted, and I had been continually mulling this main thought over and over in my mind. This thought ate at me like a cancer. The end result was a heart full of rebellion. My actions had been breeding destruction in my marriage--not healing.

I hoped the Lord would pat me on the back and say, "Oh, that's all right, Pam. I understand and love you anyway." This time, the still small voice was saying, "That's right; you can't be this kind of woman." I remember being startled and wondering for a second whether He had given up on me. Then, the Lord continued, "I can do it through you."

Those words, "I can do it through you," were very precious to me that day. I had just received a nugget from heaven. I was set free, really free, from a burden I had carried too long. If I failed, it was Jesus in me who was failing--and Jesus never fails. The Lord had become real to me. He had become personal to me. I knew what it was to enjoy the presence of my Lord and Savior. I knew I could trust Him. I was confident the Holy Spirit would empower me to do His will. My entire life was turned around when I completely placed my marriage in the Lord's hands and trusted Him to help me to become the godly woman, wife and mother He desired me to be. I remember getting up from prayer that day with complete confidence the Lord would give me all the strength and power needed to do everything He asked of me.

> *"I can do all things through Christ which strengtheneth me," (Phil. 4:13).*

It became clear to me that any good found in me or any ability or talent I possessed, all of it came from the Lord. I could take no glory. Aren't all of us infected and impure with sin? Our prized robes of righteousness are but filthy rags (Isa. 64:6).

In other words, there is no good in us. In ourselves, we are nothing. Thankfully, we serve a God who takes pleasure in making something good out of us. God has deliberately chosen to use the foolish things of this world--those things of little worth--in order to shame the wise and great. No one can brag in the presence of God.

> *"But God hath chosen the foolish things of the world to confound the wise; and God hath chosen the weak things of the world to confound the things which are mighty; And base things of the world, and things which are despised, hath God chosen, yea, and things which are not, to bring to nought things that are," (I Cor. 1:27-28).*

Does this mean that you should cower, live in defeat and believe you are worthless? Unequivocally, no. Don't ever put yourself down. You are God's creation and He loved you enough that He gave His only begotten Son, Jesus Christ, to die for you. You are His beloved child. Although you may very well be a foolish thing of this world, God has chosen the foolish things of this world to confound the wise (1 Cor. 1:27). God has taken you as His child; He has plans for your life, plans to prosper you and give you hope and a future (Jer. 29:11). God will equip you with everything good for doing His will, and He will work in you what is pleasing to Him through His Son, Jesus Christ (Heb. 13:20-21).

You have one choice, the same choice I had to make many years ago. You can either remain in the bondage of an unhappy marriage, look to God to heal your marriage or get a divorce. The choice is yours, and you have no other options. Think about it. Which choice will please God and benefit you and your family? Yield to God and choose His way. Let go and let God guide you and direct your life as you surrender to Him. Commit yourself to your marriage by doing everything the Lord shows you to do in His Word and by His Spirit to improve your marital relationship. As you obey God's Word, you, God the Father, the Lord Jesus Christ and the Holy Spirit will all be working together to save your marriage. You can search this whole world, but you will never find a more powerful or victorious team! Hallelujah!

Do you remember Abraham? When he and Sarah were told they would have a child at their advanced age, the Bible says that Abraham:

> *"...staggered not at the promise of God through unbelief; but was strong in faith, giving glory to God; And being fully persuaded that, what he had promised, he was able also to perform," (Rom. 4:20-21).*

Trust the Lord and wait on Him to complete the work He has begun in your life, your marriage and your home. Hope that is seen is not hope. When you hope for what you do not yet have, you should wait for it patiently (Rom. 8:24-25).

You may have been hoping for a long time. I cannot promise you will see immediate changes at home when you make the decision to work on your marriage. In fact, the devil will likely become angry, and things could get worse before they get better. What should you do when you are hoping and believing for something you do not see? With patience, you wait for it. You continue hoping. You continue trusting. You continue believing. You continue holding onto God's promises.

When I asked the Lord for instruction, all I heard from Him were two words, *"Trust me."* I questioned, "What are you saying to me? I need to know what to do. I need you to give me answers." When I got up from prayer, He had not given me a detailed step-by-step plan of what I should do. Neither had he given me a heads-up on what He would do. So many questions ran through my mind that long-ago day. Should I stay? Should I go? Should I seek reconciliation? Should I contact an attorney? There were so many unanswered questions. He told me to trust Him--and I am happy to report that trust in Him was enough!

> *"God is not a man, that he should lie; neither the son of man, that he should repent: hath he said, and shall he not do it? or hath he spoken, and shall he not make it good?" (Num. 23:19).*

Put your trust in Jesus and don't give up. A brighter day will come when your family will enjoy the blessings and favor of God. Your children will have both parents raising them in a loving, caring, warm Christian home. They will have strong roots to call home instead of being shuffled from pillar to post as is so often the case in today's broken homes. Your grandchildren will be strengthened by the love of both grandparents and will grow up experiencing the stability of a strong family unit.

The influence of the family unit during childhood remains with children throughout their entire lives. The Word of God is always true. God promises if we train them correctly, they will not depart (Prov. 22:6).

However, if they are not trained according to the Word of God, there is a negative side to this truth. This is why many children are exact duplicates of their parents' mistakes. Parents transmit their characteristics to their children, both good and bad. If a parent believes that divorce is right, when their children grow up and face family problems, they yield to divorce rather than God's Word a large percentage of the time. Why? Mom and Dad did it. They mistakenly conclude, "Mom and Dad couldn't make their marriage work either."

You may disagree or feel this comment is an exaggeration of truth. In my life, it is true. There were those among my family and friends who considered divorce at one time or another in the midst of their marital struggles; but thankfully, they found a way to overcome. I observed marriages close to my heart. Many had difficulties. With God's help, they made decisions not to knuckle under the pressure and to fight for their marriages. They did not give up.

During our most difficult times, these overcomers gave me the added strength I needed to stick things out. I realized this was only a season in my life, and this hard time would not last forever. I trusted that this too shall pass. When I compared this season of marital difficulty to the rest of my life without the man I loved, this season seemed short. I was, therefore, more able to cope with the hurt, realizing somewhere and sometime, the pain would cease. Joy would come in the morning. God was able to give me assurance through the examples of those close to me, those who had already overcome.

What I am saying is this: If those who make up the circle of influence in your life teach you to approve of divorce as something you must accept or cannot avoid, you will not have the same privilege and advantage I did. You will not be able to draw strength from their examples. *Beware*. Their decisions to divorce may weaken your fight and your determination to save your marriage. You may be too quick to give up on a marriage God desires to heal and restore.

> *"The Lord is longsuffering, and of great mercy, forgiving iniquity and transgression, and by no means clearing the guilty, visiting the iniquity of the fathers upon the children unto the third and fourth generation,"* (Num. 14:18).

Teach your children you serve a powerful Lord. Let your children know Jesus is your source and that He makes the difference in every area of your life, including your marriage. Ask Him to move in on the scene and take full control.

Stand up and declare once and for all:

> *"Devil, you will not destroy my family. This family will stand together and we will serve God. We are more than conquerors. In Jesus name."*

Stand up to him and fight back God's way, *on your knees.*

Declare to him you are partnering with God:

> *"Devil, you have come to steal, kill, and destroy, but Jesus has come to give me life and to give it more abundantly,"*

The choice is yours. Make it count and do what is right. Trust the Lord to give you the love, forgiveness, wisdom, patience and courage to overcome the enemy and save your marriage. It is my prayer you will choose to remain married. When you put your complete trust in Him, you can look to God to move in on the scene with help. Your striving will not result in deserving His help. Instead, His help will be the direct result of believing and trusting in a compassionate, loving and faithful God who has a purpose for you and your spouse. Your husband will then have his proper place as king and priest of his home where he will feel needed and satisfied. You will be a more fulfilled woman, as you appropriately align your priorities, putting Jesus first and your husband second.

> *"Give, and it shall be given to you; good measure, pressed down, and shaken together, and running over, shall men give into your bosom. For with the same measure that ye mete withal it shall be measured to you again,"* (Luke 6:38).

Give of yourself to bless your husband. Give of your love, your time, your faith, your strength, your support, your respect, your trust, your prayers, your patience, your courage, your wisdom, your labor, your forgiveness, your kindness, your gentleness and your encouragement. You will only receive *from* your marriage as much as you are willing to put *into* your marriage. Show him you love him. Give first, expecting in faith. Blessings will return to you in more ways than you could ever dream. Put your husband's needs and wants above your own. Seek to make him a happy man. The Lord is only waiting for you to make the first move. Here are a few ideas to help you get started:

- Plan your menu according to his favorites and give him a place of honor at the table.
- Listen intently when he speaks.
- Add a little ambience with candlelight or set your table with a decorative flare.
- Make him your priority when he is home with you. In other words, don't utilize your time with him talking on the phone to someone else.
- Be happy to watch NASCAR instead of Dancing with the Stars.
- Give up the remote control.
- Give him respect and honor.

- Hide love notes where he will find them during the day.
- Take care of his errands without him having to ask you five times.
- Schedule surprises – things that are special to him.
- Always look your best for him.
- Use good personal hygiene.
- Work with him on projects when you can.
- When he arrives home, make him welcome--knock his socks off!
- Put his clothes away, neatly folded, instead of him having to rummage through a basket of wrinkled clothes to find some underwear. In other words, take care of his needs.
- Honor his wishes, which might include sticking to the budget, having something cooked to feed your family, keeping the car clean, etc.
- Clean your house. A woman is 100% responsible for setting the atmosphere in her home. Make it pleasant, a place your husband can enjoy.
- Most importantly, give him praise.

It might surprise you to find out how often your everyday thoughts and comments give preference to self over your husband. Your answer may be found by performing a simple self-examination. Keep a notebook close by for one month and take note of which person your daily thoughts prefer: *self* or *husband*. Don't cheat.

For example, I may want scrambled eggs for breakfast, but I know my husband prefers omelets. If I say, "I am cooking scrambled eggs" with no consideration of my husband, I preferred self. If I say, instead, "Here's an omelet, your favorite," I preferred my husband. Let's look at some other examples.

SELF FIRST	HUSBAND FIRST
"I want to vacation in the mountains."	"You love riding the waves. Why don't we go to the Gulf?"
"I want to relax."	"I had a little extra time today, so I ironed your shirts. I like you to look nice."
"Let's go shopping."	"It's your day off. Won't it be great to spend a day together? What would you like for us to do?"
"I'm tired. I'd like to take a nap."	"Honey, why don't you take a few minutes to relax?"
"I do not like this restaurant."	"Let's go here. Don't you like their steaks?"
"Wait till tomorrow."	"I'll take care of this now. I know you need it."
"Serve yourself. I worked all day too, you know."	"Sit down, honey, I'll get that. You are tired, and you worked hard all day."
"I want a new car. I'll use my money if you say no."	"How do you feel about buying a new car? Can we afford it?"

Ask the Holy Spirit to help you recognize how many times your own wants and desires take first place over his. Preferring your husband with a good attitude can bring about an immediate improvement in your home.

Don't be hardheaded or controlled by pride. One of you must make the first move. Let that person be you. If you are waiting for him to make the first move, you may be waiting a very long time. Again, you have to make a choice. What will it be? Humble yourself and be the vessel God can use to save your marriage. Let God use you.

Determine in your heart and mind you will stand and fight for your marriage. Refuse to run. Commit yourself to begin working on your marriage immediately, casting down any imaginations or fantasies you may have regarding a new life without him. God is in the healing business. He is more than able to redeem your troubled marriage.

Women who are submitted to God, walking in God's wisdom, and obedient to His Word will experience God's power. Jesus will lead them every step of the way.

Foolish women who rebelliously do their own thing, however, will destroy their homes (Prov. 14:1). All their power and energies will achieve negative results.

It is important to realize women hold a powerful position in their homes. They can either promote the building and restoration of their homes and families, or they can be instrumental in their destruction. Don't allow the enemy of your soul to steal and destroy your family's future. Instead, seek God for ways to improve your home, marriage and family, improvements which will carry over to future generations.

Restoration and healing are serious business, and you need to take your marriage seriously. We are talking about devoting your time to *saving* and *restoring* your home, marriage and family. Aren't you thankful God is a restorer? He will give you all the wisdom you need to restore your home and marriage. He is always ready to give you a bountiful supply of wisdom. When you ask Him, expect Him to give you a solid answer. Don't be tossed by the wind, filled with doubt and uncertainty (James 1:5-8). You serve a faithful God who loves you and cares about every need you have, including your need for a better marriage (1 Pet. 5:7).

As you ask the Lord to heal your marriage and as you approach Him with a pure heart and with pure motives, the Lord will not turn you away. His hand is outstretched to heal your home.

Many of your fights and quarrels come from the desires that battle within you, wanting something but not getting it. You don't have because you have not asked God--or you are asking with wrong motives.

> *"From whence come wars and fightings among you? Come they not hence, even of your lusts that war in your members? Ye lust, and have not; ye kill, and desire to have, and cannot obtain: ye fight and war, yet ye have not, because ye ask not. Ye ask, and receive not, because ye ask amiss, that ye may consume it upon your lusts," (James 4:1-3).*

This may sound hard, but this is what God says. I have no doubt your agony of decision is stressful. Your health can also be negatively affected during this arduous time. It doesn't have to be this way.

I pray you have been inspired, motivated and stirred by the Holy Spirit. I pray your heart has been filled with determination to commit your *all* to the Lord and to your marital relationship.

Make a decision now that will reverse the enemy's attacks, a decision that will *cancel* his destructive plans for your home and family. Look ahead to the future! God has a better future planned for you, filled with blessings and purpose. Don't turn away! He is waiting for you to call on

Him. Only Jesus can do the impossible in your life and marriage. He is *able*!

When all is coming against you, when all hope is gone, when your situation looks impossible, choose Jesus!

Stop procrastinating. It is decision time.

CHAPTER SIX
ARISE! SHINE!

"Arise, shine, for thy light is come, and the glory of the Lord is risen upon thee," (Isa. 60:1).

This is what God is saying to you today. This is basically the same thing Jesus spoke to blind Bartimaeus (Mark 10:46-52).

Remember Bartimaeus, the blind man who sat by the highway side begging for money. When he heard that Jesus of Nazareth was passing by, he began to cry out, *"Jesus, thou son of David, have mercy on me."* Many wanted him to hold his peace, but he only cried louder. Jesus asked him, *"What wilt thou that I should do unto thee?"* And Bartimaeus answered, *"Lord, that I might receive my sight."*

"And Jesus said unto him, Go thy way; thy faith hath made thee whole. And immediately he received his sight, and followed Jesus in the way," (Mark 10:52).

How long do you think Bartimaeus sat by the roadside begging? Can you imagine the hopelessness he felt believing he would never see? Can you imagine the dreams that had died in his heart? Can you imagine the despair he experienced, knowing life was passing him by? Do you think he might have given up? Do you think his heart was filled with pain feeling like nobody cared about him?

What about you? Have you given up? Do you feel life is passing you by? God best shows His magnificent power when we are in our deepest, darkest times of despair. That is exactly what happened to Bartimaeus. Jesus gave sight to a blind man, renewing his life and giving him hope for a better future.

I can imagine the dreams that have gone to sleep within your heart. Over time, you have no doubt given up on many things you have so desired. I see Jesus calling to you to rise and be healed. He wants to set your faith loose so you can see the possibility of abundant life ahead for both you and those you love.

Maybe you blame the devil, or your husband, or even yourself for the pain in your marriage. Worse than that, you may blame God. Your hurt may have been caused by circumstances totally out of your control. Possibly, some of the responsibility lies with you. The Lord receives no glory out of you being in this hopeless, depressed and discouraged state of mind.

Bartimaeus begged on the roadside for money, but was money what he really needed? No. He needed Jesus. Regretfully, you may have reached out in some wrong area-- drugs, alcohol, etc.--to satisfy your pain. Bartimaeus tried reaching out to many passersby. Could man meet his need?

No. In your pain, you may have reached out to friends, family or church leaders--desperate to find relief. Neither money nor man could meet the need in the life of Bartimaeus. Yet, when Bartimaeus cried out to Him, Jesus did the impossible and healed his sight.

> "…With men it is impossible, but not with God: for with God all things are possible," (Mark 10:27).

Jesus of Nazareth gave Bartimaeus a new life. The glory came when Bartimaeus cried out to Jesus in faith for his sight. He miraculously walked away a new man.

Bartimaeus cried. Jesus heard and bid him to come. In the same way, Jesus has heard the cries of your heart. He is bidding for you to come to Him. He wants to lift you up from your depths of despair. Are you blind like Bartimaeus, surviving in your circumstances and seeing no way things can improve? You too shall live again. You too shall be energized by the Spirit of God. You too shall have purpose in God's kingdom. The Lord is not going to let you bury and hide from the world because of what you have been through. He's not going to let you wallow around in self-pity and settle for a life of pain. No. I know you believe your life is harder and your marriage is more difficult than those around you. It's time for that "stinking thinking" to end. Jesus is ready to raise you up, heal your hurt and give you purpose. All you have to do is put your faith and trust in Him.

The people told blind Bartimaeus, *"Be of good comfort, rise; he calleth thee."* He listened. His faith and obedience resulted in the restoration of his sight and life.

Blindness had Bartimaeus bound. What might have you bound? By faith, command those things to let you go in Jesus' name.

HOPELESSNESS	Depart in Jesus' name!
PAIN & GRIEF	Depart in Jesus' name!
SELF-PITY	Depart in Jesus' name!
DISCOURAGEMENT	Depart in Jesus' name!
FEAR	Depart in Jesus' name!

Now rise up! Begin walking into your new and exciting future. The Lord has great things in store for you. The Word says *"the violent take it by force"* (Matt. 11:12). Take the kingdom of God with earnestness. Forcefully come against sin and those satanic powers that attempt to compromise your faith. Stand true even when things get hard. Pursue those promises that God has for you. Don't allow the enemy to destroy your life, marriage and family.

You know your adversary is the devil, and he is walking around as a roaring lion seeking whom he may devour (1 Pet. 5:8). His mission is to steal, kill and destroy (John 10:10). He would like to devour your marriage, your family and the church. What better place for him to begin than with you? Look to Jesus! He has overcome the world, the flesh and the devil.

Where does that put those of us who believe in Jesus Christ?

First of all, we have a promise that when the enemy comes in like a flood, the Spirit of the Lord lifts up a standard against him (Isa. 59:19). Secondly, Jesus has won the victory that overcomes the world. When we believe in Jesus Christ as the Son of God, our faith in Him makes us overcomers in this world (1 John 5:4-5).

In his devotional book, *My Utmost for His Highest*, Oswald Chambers wrote:

> *"The greatest enemy of the life of faith in God is not sin, but good choices which are not quite good enough. The good is always the enemy of the best...."*

Let's not settle for mediocrity. Let's strive for God's best. We can overcome the world and the devil through our faith in Jesus Christ by forsaking all and trusting Him.

Pray daily, calling on Jesus for help to protect, guard and keep your husband and family. Pray with the authority the Lord has given to all believers. Plead the blood of Jesus over your family and ask for God's peace to abide in your home. God answers prayer. If He hears your faintest cry, don't you think He will honor your sincere, heart-wrenching prayer?

> *"...The effectual fervent prayer of a righteous man availeth much,"* (James 5:16).

As you pray, take authority over those spirits that have your husband bound. At the same time, love your husband. Even when we were sinners, Christ loved us and died for us. Learn to hate the sin and love the sinner.

I have had the privilege of knowing some very special women of God whose husbands were unbelievers. They loved their husbands with all their hearts. They lavished them with love, showed them respect, submitted to their authority in the home and served them joyfully as unto God. These wives did not see through carnal eyes. By spending time with Jesus, they saw their husbands as Jesus saw them and they loved their husbands as Jesus loved them. These women were vessels of honor, and Jesus was able to effectively minister His love to these men through these praying, spirit-filled and obedient women of God. Jesus helped these women to be excellent wives, even while walking through their less-than-perfect circumstances. Their husbands were blessed to have them by their sides. The obstacles they faced were different in each family. We watched them walk out their faith, firmly putting their trust in Almighty God. Many years and many trials later, we saw these men turn to God. We believe they are in heaven today as a result of the unwavering love, prayers and commitment of their godly wives.

Are you showing your husband by your care and love for him that you walk with God?

> *"Yea, a man may say, Thou hast faith, and I have works: shew me thy faith without thy works, and I will shew thee my faith by my works. Thou believest that there is one God; thou doest well; the devils also believe, and tremble. But wilt thou know, O vain man, that faith without works is dead?" (James 2:18-20).*

Your struggle is not with your spouse, but against the spiritual forces of evil and powers of this dark world that have him bound. Trust the Lord. Don't get caught in the trap of responding to the negative circumstances around you. Rise above them. Focus your eyes on Jesus Christ. Dig into God's Word. Be sensitive to the Spirit of God and obedient to the Lord's voice. Leave the rest to Him.

You are only responsible for what the Lord requires of you. Your husband must answer for himself. You must resist the temptation to lead, control, correct or instruct your husband. This is not your responsibility. Realize your freedom from trying to be his mother. You are not. Realize your freedom from trying to be his Holy Spirit. You are not. Realize your freedom from trying to be his teacher. You are not. Realize your freedom from trying to be your husband's covering by hiding or covering his sin. You are not. Love does cover a multitude of sins. There are, however, those times when the Lord may choose to expose everything done in secret. Though these times may be humbling and painful for all concerned, you are not at all responsible. Be set free of these burdens. They are not yours to carry. In fact, should this happen, be encouraged the Lord is at work in your marriage and in your husband's life. The Lord always disciplines His children out of a heart of love.

The *principle of harvest* indicates:

- What we feed grows.
- What we starve dies.

Most often, once sin is exposed, it ceases to be fed. Therefore, the sin will die. Be brave, and trust the Lord to work in your husband's life. The Lord knows exactly what is required to purge sin.

During this difficult and stressful time, devote yourself to *feeding* your marital relationship by:

- Loving your husband with all your heart.
- Praying for your spouse daily with diligence and consistency.

Get ready and keep your eyes of faith open.

Believe for your miracle!

LORD, HEAL OUR MARRIAGE

CHAPTER SEVEN
A SUBMITTED LIFE
(A BATTLE ON YOUR KNEES)

Submission is an action word, one that brings life, not death. It is not a curse word. Jesus willingly submitted to the Father, though He was just as much a part of the Godhead. Submitting to your husband does not make you inferior to him. In fact, the two of you are *"heirs together of the grace of life"* (1 Pet. 3:7). You and your husband are partners in receiving the blessings of God. Your husband's prayers will not get ready answers if he does not treat you as he should.

Is submission necessary in our lives? The Word of God clearly teaches believers are to submit to the following: to God; to the laws of man; the younger to elders; to all true workers; to one another; to those who rule over us; and wives to their husbands.

The Lord will never ask or command us to do anything that is not for our own good. Submission has become a "dirty" word in today's society. When we hear it, it speaks death. Hearing the word "submission" usually brings out the worst in us. Does the "S" word immediately cause you to become defensive or angry? Do not feel alone. If you have the same mindset I once had regarding submission, you probably cringe at the very sound of the word.

Years ago, neither my husband nor I was a born-again believer. I had secretly scheduled an appointment with an attorney to file for divorce. Prior to the appointment, I was invited to a revival service where an altar worker handed me a New Testament. As I flipped the Bible open, there it was. A Scripture verse seemed to jump off the page at me in big, bold letters. I was certain God was trying to get my attention. Being filled with curiosity, I asked one of the altar workers to explain verse ten, and she took the time to explain the entire seventh chapter of 1st Corinthians to me. This is what God's Word said to me the night I gave my heart to Jesus:

> *"And unto the married I command, yet not I, but the Lord, Let not the wife depart from her husband," (1 Cor. 7:10).*

Now, it doesn't get any plainer than this. I was very strong-willed, but I still clearly understood these words. I was married, and "Do not leave your husband" was God's message to me. The Bible was a new addition to my reading material, so I am positive I could not have found this particular Scripture verse on my own had I searched for it for hours. I felt like God unlocked the door to my innermost secret. God knew that I was planning to file for divorce. How? No one knew. A certain amount of fear gripped me when I realized nothing was hid from Almighty God (Prov. 15:3). I decided I better pay attention, obey God and give Him a try. Early the next morning, I cancelled my appointment with the attorney, never to meet with him or call his office again.

Our marriage did not become dreamy overnight, and patience has never been my strongest virtue. Regrettably, I had already written my marriage off in my heart, giving little room for hope. As a result, the poor attitude I possessed required a miracle from God to convince me there was any possibility my marriage could survive. Having little faith, I asked God for a child to be that sign. It sounds foolish now to think I was ready to divorce my husband, and yet, was praying for a child. Nevertheless, that's where I was at the time. I was asking for such a miraculous sign for one reason--to know God was in complete control. I needed this powerful confirmation from Him. We had been trying to have a baby for three years. I had already submitted to several medical tests and had taken various fertility drugs, all to no avail. Did God give me my miracle?

I was saved on October 18, 1977. To my surprise, just before Thanksgiving, I found out I was pregnant. Ten months after I gave my heart to the Lord, my son was born. As a young Christian, I was awestruck at the way the Lord answered my prayer. I was confident that this was God's confirmation to me to stay married to my husband. I had no doubt this baby was a special gift from heaven in direct response to my prayer that night at the altar.

Many months later, my husband still was not saved. I had prayed and prayed for God to change him. It just wasn't happening. I was losing heart, and discouragement was beginning to set in. Before I believed in Jesus Christ, my marriage was struggling to survive. Now, instead of our marriage getting better, it was growing worse. It seemed we were traveling in opposite directions. Shouldn't our marriage have improved now that I was a born-again believer? I didn't understand.

Several more months passed. One day, I sat in a Sunday school class where the subject of submission was being discussed. I sat biting my lips with my fists clenched, and I could not sit still. I wiggled in my seat and constantly glanced at my watch waiting for the bell to ring that would end the class. It was easy to understand how this sweet, precious teacher, who was the personification of meekness, could submit. She did not go home with me. She was not walking in my shoes or living in my house. She could not possibly understand. Her husband was a Christian, so there was no way this teacher could relate to my disappointments, much less tell me what I should do.

It was not that my husband did not take care of me. Please understand he has always been a very hard worker and an excellent provider. To others, he seemed to be a terrific husband. In the world's eyes, he seemed better than most. However, I had become weary of dealing with the consequences of his ungodly choices. I was the one feeling the effects of those choices. Regardless, was I so perfect that God appointed me his judge? I don't think so.

Before the class came to an end, I left. I picked up my purse and dashed out, slamming the door closed behind me. My ugly spirit was definitely putting on a show. Anger could not even begin to describe the way I felt. My insides boiled. The class ended; thankfully, the Holy Spirit had only begun. It seemed the words I heard would not go away. They bothered me. My mind would hit replay all day and night. Up to this point, everything I had heard contradicted the way I lived and challenged what I believed. The words that had been spoken penetrated deeply into my heart. Though I tried hard to brush them aside, I could not.

I joined my husband for an out-of-town trip and spent the day in the motel room while he worked. This gave me ample time to read, pray and seek the Lord. I set out on a specific mission. I purposed in my heart to prove wrong everything I had heard about submission. It had to be wrong. No wife should have to submit to her husband. It was not fair. I was determined to find the truth, and I couldn't wait to see what God really said about the topic of submission in His Word.

> "Shew me thy ways, O Lord; teach me thy paths. Lead me in thy truth, and teach me: for thou art the God of my salvation; on thee do I wait all the day," (Psalms 25:4-5).

My haughty attitude did not change the fact submission is not a request from God, but it is a *command* to wives. Once I discovered the truth, I had a responsibility to *conform* to it. I had to repent. Whether you agree or disagree, your opinion will not change the fact God's Word is true and does not change. The bottom line, ladies, is we *must* submit to our husbands as unto the Lord. There's no other way.

Often a concept or principle can be better understood by studying the opposite. The *opposite of submit* means to:

- Resist or exert force in opposition.
- Oppose with firm determination and rebel.

Therefore, it became very clear to me if I refused to submit, if I continued to resist, and if I remained determined to oppose, I would be living in rebellion. God leaves no gray area when it comes to submission. The fight I had going on inside me was a rebellion that did not please God.

Submitting to a husband who loves you as Christ loves the church is wonderfully ideal. What do you do when you are struggling to live with the real? How do you overcome? How do you obey? How do you yield to anything less than godly love from your husband? Is it possible? Let me say, yes, it is possible. You have a perfect example, Jesus Christ. His life was far from ideal. Yet, He gave us the plan to victory by teaching us submission.

Picture a step ladder in your mind. At the top of this ladder, there is wealth, fame, power and all that success has to offer in this life. In the world's eyes, you must climb *up* the ladder to acquire victory. Every step higher would mean you were advancing in power and stature. Every step up would take you a little closer to making your mark, receiving your promotion or winning your prize. In the business world, many people give little consideration to how far they are willing to go or how many people they are willing to hurt while climbing their ladders to success, power and greatness.

Jesus teaches us His ways are not like ours; His ways are higher. He teaches us that, unlike the world, the way to true victory is not necessarily up. As far as we are concerned, when we follow His example, it seems our steps are taking us *down* the ladder. Jesus teaches humility; therefore, we often feel we are losing ground. In reality, are we?

> *"Humble yourselves therefore under the mighty hand of God, that he may exalt you in due time,"* (1 Pet. 5:6).

What do you think it means to live a submitted life? Let's look closely at how Jesus prayed in the Garden of Gethsemane.

> *"...O my Father, if it be possible, let this cup pass from me: nevertheless not as I will, but as thou wilt."* (Matt. 26:39).

Jesus prayed, *"My Father."* Jesus knew His Father. He called Him *"My Father,"* showing ownership and that a personal relationship existed between the two of them. He shared His need with His Father. He asked for relief, showing the communion they had with each other. Jesus had learned who His Father really was. He had learned of His Father's character. He had learned of His Father's love. Most of all, He had learned He could trust in that love.

If you are to comprehend submission, you must first develop a personal relationship with Jesus Christ. You must have confidence in His love toward you. You must know He is looking out for your best interest in every situation you face. You must know His Word is true. You must completely trust Him. You must understand His power to move your mountains. You ask, "Can I have such a relationship with Jesus?" Yes, you can. The more time you spend with Him, the more you will understand His power, His character, His faithfulness and His love.

"Nevertheless, not as I will," is a good depiction of His surrender to His Father. Jesus agonized until his sweat turned to blood. Jesus counted the cost. Yet, even though He knew His destiny would be to die on the Cross, He chose to surrender to His Father's will. He chose to surrender to a higher purpose. What might have you prayed had you been in His shoes? My dialogue with the Father might have sounded more like this: "Father, can't you see these people have mistreated me; these people don't deserve my help; these people rejected me? Can't you see that I have not sinned and I don't deserve to die this way?"

Instead, Jesus chose to commit and yield to His Father's will and was not ruled by circumstances. To walk in submission, you must lay aside your own will. You must yield to a greater purpose. Give up self and allow the Lord to direct you through His Word and by His Spirit. Surrender and make the Lord's will your priority. Have you willingly surrendered your will? Is there still a fight going on inside you?

My Sunday school teacher shared a story he'd heard on Dr. James Dobson's "Focus on the Family" radio program. The story went something like this. A young boy was punished by his teacher and told to kneel in the corner. The child reluctantly walked over to the corner. As he knelt down, he looked back at his teacher with a frown. The little boy told him, "I might be kneeling on the outside, but on the inside, I am really standing up."

There are times we reluctantly surrender and act. Nevertheless, our hearts are still standing up in rebellion, demanding their own way. Like the little boy, our hearts are not in agreement with our actions. In marriage, we must willfully give up our individual rights and surrender our wills in order to submit to our husbands as unto Christ. Therefore, you must pray, as Jesus did, until you can completely surrender your will to another. Please understand your unconditional obedience is to Jesus. He can be trusted. Allow Jesus to lead and direct you.

This does not include obedience to a perverted husband, of course. A minister friend [we will call her Grace] asked me to share her personal testimony. Her desire is to help women who might be living her story. As a young girl, Grace married a man controlled by sexual sin and the desires of the flesh. This man's lustful activities began with his insistence that his wife join him in the viewing of pornography. His perverted desires progressed and later expanded to wanting her to share their marriage bed to include other women. Can you see why Grace's obedience to either request would have been disobedience to God's Word?

In a marriage where sexual sin is involved, a series of events are necessary to bring about healing in a marriage. First, there must be genuine repentance. Secondly, forgiveness must follow. Lastly, God's healing power completes the restoration process which is only made possible through forgiveness. True healing and restoration will never take place in a marriage apart from true repentance; without repentance, there can be no forgiveness of sin. In this marriage, Grace's husband refused to repent and he moved out, even after being given many opportunities for reconciliation. Grace could not submit to his sinful demands. Unfortunately, Grace's marriage ended in divorce. Thankfully, God restored Grace's life. Years later, He sent her a godly husband, and the two of them have been serving together in ministry for many years.

If your husband attempts to lead you away from Jesus Christ, he no longer qualifies as your spiritual husband. Jesus Himself becomes your spiritual husband. Your husband can never be your God. Putting him before your God is idolatry. If you choose to follow your husband rather than Jesus, you are pushing Jesus out of your life and rejecting His help. The Father, the Son and the Holy Spirit will no longer be working with you to restore your marriage. You will be on your own, doing things your way. Never forget that in order to receive life from the vine, you must stay *attached* to the vine. Jesus is the True Vine.

> *"I am the vine, ye are the branches; He that abideth in me, and I in him, the same bringeth forth much fruit; for without me ye can do nothing," (John 15:5).*

As Jesus prayed, *"As thou wilt,"* He made a conscious decision to obey and yield to His Father's will. Obedience was His personal choice. He surrendered His will, and followed through, ultimately paying the price. You must make the choice to obey. No one can make that choice for you. Will you allow the Lord to work through you to touch your husband's heart? Will you be a yielded vessel for the Holy Spirit to flow through?

Jesus trusted His Father, not His circumstances. You must trust that the Lord not only knows what is best for you, but He will also do what is best in your life. When we have that kind of faith and desire to fulfill His purpose in our lives, we can confidently trust the Lord to work all things together for our good (Rom. 8:28).

Jesus set an example of silent obedience (Matt. 26:63). He did not defend Himself, nor was He argumentative. He kept His peace. There is something extraordinary about knowing you are right with God and walking in obedience to Him that brings peace even in the midst of turmoil. Knowing He loves you and cares for you gives you the courage you will need to completely obey His Word.

I went through a period many years ago where the Lord was teaching me obedience. If anyone needed a lesson in submission and obedience, I did. A test will always come with growth. This particular test came in the form of a request from my husband. He asked me to put a hold on spending during an upcoming pay period. Wouldn't you know my phone would ring that very night? It was my girlfriend asking me to join her for one of the largest sales of the year. Naturally, I said yes, but I made a promise to myself I would only window shop and not spend any money.

Now, I wear a size 4½ ladies' shoe which is difficult to find. A store we strolled through had beautiful name-brand shoes on sale for $10 a pair. These same shoes sold for $50 to $65 a pair, or more, and there were three pair in my size! With shoes in my size so hard to find and at $10 a pair, wouldn't I be sorry in the long run? My husband knew how difficult it was for me to find shoes that fit. He would approve of the price. If I called him, I was positive he'd agree I should purchase them. Surely, I could justify at least one pair. I knew he would understand. Then again, at $10 a pair, should I even tell him? I could always stuff them in my closet and bring them out at a later date. He'd never know. My girlfriend aided and abetted by offering to loan me the money saying I could pay her back when things weren't so tight.

As I tried them on and admired them in the mirror, I kept hearing the last request my husband had made of me. As I put them on and took them off several times, there was no doubt a war going on in the spiritual realm--and it had to do with my obedience. Realizing this, I put the shoes down and quickly walked out of the store. Staring at me in disbelief, my girlfriend wondered, "Is she really going to pass up this great sale?"

I was overjoyed with victory on the way home because I knew I made the right choice. Obedience felt great. I had willfully yielded to my husband's wishes instead of seeking my own way. I could have put up a fight. I worked and had my own money to spend. We'd always pooled our money and did not live by the "his" and "hers" plan. I didn't mention a word about the shoes to my husband. As far as I was concerned, it was a private matter between me, the Lord and my friend. He knew I went shopping. Although he made no comment, I could tell he was pleasantly surprised when I returned home with no shopping bags. Yes, I did catch him looking.

However, my story did not end there. At 8:15 the next morning, our doorbell rang. No one usually visited us that early in the morning. I answered the door and was surprised to find an elderly lady from our church, fondly called Mom Treadaway, standing on our front porch. She was one of our most highly respected prayer warriors. I had never known anyone quite like her. She had a very large family and believed strongly in the power of prayer. Today, many of her children are involved in ministry. Over the years, I was privileged to attend several overnight prayer meetings she led for our church ladies. She was instrumental in teaching me how to *"lay hold to the horns of the altar."* In other words, with a pure, contrite and humble heart, keep praying until the answer comes.

She began to explain her reason for stopping by. She had cleaned out some vacant apartments for someone, including one where the tenant had skipped town without paying the rent. The tenant had left behind a closet full of shoes. There was every type of shoe, many brand new with price tags still attached. They were all the small size of 4 ½. She said when she saw shoes for such petite feet, she didn't know of anyone who wore that size. She started to drop them by Goodwill. In her habit of praying about everything, she asked the Lord. She said the Lord told her to drop the shoes off at my house. Since I worked at the church, she assumed I might come across or know of someone with small feet who needed them, never dreaming the Lord was blessing me for my obedience. I knew! Because she was sensitive to the Holy Spirit and obedient to the Lord, God was able to bless me as well as teach me a life-changing lesson. [This confirms that God does not always immediately reveal His full plan. When He leads you to do something, He may only be giving you one piece of the puzzle. God had given Mom Treadaway the "what" to do, but had not given her the "why."] Instead of buying one pair of shoes one day in disobedience, I received twenty-eight pairs of shoes the next day, including eight brand new pairs, as a result of my obedience. This girl learned a powerful lesson regarding the blessings of obedience.

I want you to know this one incident changed my life forever. This was no coincidence. God had my full attention. My hope He would notice my obedience became a sure reality. Jesus truly cared about me and something as insignificant as shoes. He knew my thoughts and could read my heart. This brought God's love for me to a level I could receive and understand, and other similar instances followed. I learned in a very personal way that all God required of me was to be obedient to Him and submit to His authority. Obedience is all He requires of you, too. He is no respecter of persons. He will take care of you. He is not only concerned with your needs, but if you delight yourself in Him, He will give you the desires of your heart (Psalms 37:4).

Another incident happened when I was driving my elderly mother and aunt to a funeral service in Kenner, Louisiana. Suddenly, my station wagon had a blow-out, and I was in a critical place on the interstate, directly in the center of heavy traffic. I was able to safely maneuver the car from the passing lane of I-10 to the shoulder of the highway. I had just gotten out of the vehicle and swung open the rear door of the station wagon, when a pickup truck pulled up behind me. It was a good friend from Chalmette, Louisiana. I was at least 45 miles from home and was thankful to see a familiar face when I needed help. The used station wagon was new to us, so I knew very little about the vehicle and could offer little help to Rene' as he searched for the tire tool and such. For some reason, the tire tool in the station wagon did not fit. He checked to see if the one on his truck might fit, and it didn't either. He then remembered someone at his salvage yard had thrown a tire tool in the back of his pickup. Guess what? It was the precise tire tool he needed to change my tire. It fit perfectly. God had provided the help and exact tool I needed at the specific time I needed it. Coincidence? No way! Once again, I recognized God's hand at work in my life. Rene' put on my spare tire, and I proceeded to the funeral home with the ladies.

Immediately after the funeral service, I called my husband at his office. I explained how I planned to purchase a new tire at a tire dealership across the street from the funeral home. I had already priced the tire and was just calling to tell him what had happened. I had it all under control. Did I really? My husband instructed me to handle the situation differently. He did not want me to purchase a tire from that store. Instead, he insisted that I take the station wagon to a dealership about twenty miles away. It didn't make sense to me. Why go the extra distance on a spare? As I was speaking to him, I was looking out the funeral home window at the store directly across the street. Why was he being so difficult? I then remembered the shoes.

Puzzled at his response, I loaded up my mom and aunt and drove to the tire store of his choice. They measured the tread on the tire and told me the tire was defective. They put a brand new tire on the station wagon, and they only charged me $6. Now his request made sense. I realized my husband knew something I didn't know. I would have spent well over $100 for the same thing. Once again, I learned a valuable lesson regarding the blessings of obedience.

As you obey God, you may not always have a support team. My elderly mom and aunt were tired and wanted to get home. They were worried about driving on a spare. They wanted me to take the car across the street from the funeral home. What if the spare was no good and we didn't make it to the other tire store? Jesus, too, did not have a support team, and he could not depend on his friends. Even when He asked His disciples (those closest to Him) to pray, they fell asleep. They meant well, but they were no support. His disciples slept when He needed them most (Matt. 26:36-45).

Others may not fully understand what the Lord is doing in your life. My mom and aunt had no clue God was trying to teach me submission and obedience that day. In the same way, Peter meant well when he stepped out in the Lord's defense and slashed off the right ear of Malchus, the High Priest's servant (John 18:10-11). Peter was only doing what he thought was right and did not know he was interfering with God's plan. Often, you will find those closest to you mean well, but they may get in the way and unknowingly interfere with God's will for you. Don't be surprised if you have to walk without human company or affirmation. You will not be alone. God will never leave you nor forsake you (Deut. 31:6).

Jesus took another step down the ladder of humility when He prayed, *"Father, forgive them for they know not what they do."* Jesus understood that a sinner is blind. A sinner usually has no idea of the damage his sinful life will have on others. If your husband is living in sin, he may be blind to the fact his sins are hurting you. Sinners convince themselves the effects or consequences of their sins will hurt no one but themselves. Sinners are also deceived into believing what others don't know won't hurt them. Of course, this is a falsehood.

Jesus taught His disciples to forgive (Matt 6:14-15). We must release those who have hurt us (John 20:23). Un-forgiveness will harm you as well as those you harbor it against.

> <u>UN-FORGIVENESS</u> - CAUSES BONDAGE FOR THE SINNER AND SICKNESS FOR THE ONE WHO WAS HURT.
>
> <u>FORGIVENESS</u> - RELEASES AND SETS THE SINNER FREE AND BRINGS HEALING TO THE ONE WHO WAS HURT.

Years ago, a friend shared a Mark Twain's quote with our class which she had read in an Ann Lander's column. It was worth remembering:

> *"Anger is an acid that does more harm to the vessel in which it is stored than to anything on which it is poured."*

The same goes for hatred and un-forgiveness. I had to forgive my husband numerous times, often for the same thing. It is very disappointing to see someone you love fall into sin over and over again. Straddling the fence made him easy prey for the enemy. I questioned whether he would ever totally commit his life to the Lord. I questioned whether I was wasting my time and prayers. I questioned whether he was taking my love for granted. Most of all, I questioned whether he was taking Jesus for granted. Nevertheless, as I observed Jesus forgive him over and over again, I realized Jesus was not finished with him yet. This gave me hope for a better future.

Even as a non-believer, in most areas, my husband was a very good man. I had faith to believe whenever he truly committed his life to Jesus, he would be a terrific husband. It was obvious Jesus was still working in his life. Therefore, the main role I could play in reaching him was allowing forgiveness to flow from my heart to his. He needed to see Jesus in me. Make no mistake. This was no easy task. Today, my husband is a man of integrity and highly respected among his peers. Most of all, he is a man I hold in high esteem. He has my utmost respect and trust. This is a true work of God in our lives.

Are you still holding grievances in your heart against your husband? Release him. Set him free. Give him life. Look through eyes of faith. Be healed in Jesus' name.

Jesus didn't look through eyes of defeat. His hope was just beyond the horizon. He looked past, around and over His circumstances. Like a running back, He saw beyond His obstacles. He saw the goal line and the victory ahead. He envisioned Himself seated at the right hand of His Father and coming in the clouds of glory (Matt. 26:64).

What are you envisioning? Can you see your marriage whole? Stay focused on a God who is not only able to work, but one who is presently at work in your marriage. Don't lose sight of the goal line. Your help comes from Jesus (Psa. 121:1-8).

Have you ever felt forsaken by God and ended up murmuring and complaining? Death to self is crushingly painful; it never comes easy for us. Do you think it was easy for Jesus?

> *"And about the ninth hour Jesus cried with a loud voice, saying, Eli, Eli, lama sabachthani? That is to say, My God, my God, why hast thou forsaken me?"* (Matt 27:46).

God's grace will empower you to fulfill God's will in your life. Jesus was not forced to die. He willingly died. Ironically, His death won Him the victory.

In the same way, dying to self will never accomplish what it is meant to accomplish if it is forced. You must *willingly* lay down your life. This is the secret to becoming more Christ-like. You will be on your way to becoming a stronger woman of faith. You must seek Jesus and His truth first; then, strip those things out of your life you know to be wrong, those lusts and desires which have sprung from delusion [DELUSION -- BELIEFS HELD WITH STRONG CONVICTION DESPITE SUPERIOR EVIDENCE TO THE CONTRARY], even those ideas you have clung to in your past. With a fresh attitude, you will put on those things you know to be right, which will better reveal your new life of holiness (Eph. 4:21-24).

Sometimes, we make changes in our lives in compliance with a fresh, new understanding of God's Word. Basically, we hear the truth, immediately yield to the truth, and repent. Other times, changes are the result of repentance after long-term rebellion and disobedience, where we held on tight to our old ways even when we knew they were wrong. Jesus calls this *sin* when we knew the right thing to do, but refused to do it (James 4:17).

For example, there were times I knew I owed my husband an apology. It may have been for saying a sharp or flippant remark or for having a bad attitude. It was definitely a pride issue. I outright refused to say I was sorry because of the pride in my heart. Pride is the opposite of humility. My dad raised me to believe saying "I'm sorry" was a sign of weakness. I was taught to look someone square in their eyes and never show weakness. I was strong, I was a Dupuy, and I was proud of it.

Even when I knew apologizing was the right thing to do, I still absolutely refused to do it. This was sin. It was nearly five years into my marriage before I would even begin to do what I knew to be right all along, to say "I am sorry." Even then, an apology didn't come easy. I chokingly spewed those words from my mouth. My former nature, my old self, my flesh, my own will, did not give up without a fight. My flesh did not want to die. Neither shall yours. Wisdom gained through age and experience has taught me to say "I'm sorry" even when it seems difficult to do so. Give no room for the enemy to set up camp in your heart or in your husband's heart. As the will of God wins out and brings about death to your will, your new nature will spring forth. It is at this point where Christian character is developed.

Jesus obediently set His own will aside when He laid down His life. He did His part. The Father did not let it end with death. Hallelujah! Jesus experienced God's resurrection power, and He came out of the grave. Death lost its power. Death lost its grip. Jesus is alive and He holds the keys to death, hell and the grave. All authority is given Him by His Father, and victory is complete. Jesus Himself said, *"It is finished"* (John 19:30).

In the same way, *"your old self"* may die, but *"your new self"* will rise with power, strength and a renewed mind and spirit. You will hardly be able to contain your excitement as His power works through you, and He uses you to touch the lives of others, especially your husband.

This is the victory: Once you have survived death [and you will survive], you will find death had no real victory. Death had no real sting. You may have received a few scars along the way, but Jesus took away all the pain. The devil lost His power over you. Everything the devil meant for your destruction, Jesus turned around for your good. You have overcome through Him!

For the thief comes to steal, kill and destroy. Jesus came so that you could have an abundant and overflowing life (John 10:10). He promises to "*restore to you the years that the locust hath eaten, the cankerworm, and the caterpillar and the palmerworm*" (Joel 2:25).

I once felt I was slipping down the steps of the ladder of life and losing ground. I felt I was hanging onto the ladder with all my strength, refusing to relinquish any more ground by taking another step down. The devil was screaming to me, "You're a loser!" The world was screaming to me, "Submit? Are you crazy?" The entire time, I was screaming, "Ouch! This hurts! Lord, where are you?" Nothing had gone unnoticed by the Lord. I promise you are not a loser. He sees all you are going through, and He loves you. God opposes the proud, but He gives grace to the humble (James 4:6). You may feel very insignificant now, but He promises to lift you up and make your life important and meaningful (James 4:10). You have a divine destiny ahead.

You are *not* a loser. If you exalt yourself in pride, you will be shutting God out of your life and marriage. You will be pushing the Lord away and refusing His help. Humbling yourself before God and submitting to His Word will never make you a loser. To the contrary, humility and obedience will put you in a position to receive God's greatest rewards. You will be a winner. You will have God's best. All of His promises will be yours. You will not be alone. The power of the Godhead will be with you, and God's mighty power will be working on your behalf.

Battling on your knees will give you firsthand experience of God's amazing resurrection power--*the victory of a submitted life.*

Hindsight is always 20/20. Now, I can look back and see Jesus around every curve, around every corner, and beside me in every step I had to take. Jesus had been with me the entire time. He had been with me during every struggle.

"God is our refuge and strength, a very present help in trouble," (Psa. 46:1).

Look for Jesus. He is no respecter of persons.

CHAPTER EIGHT
YOKED TOGETHER FOR A PURPOSE

Close your eyes and try your best to imagine two oxen joined by a yoke.

Webster's dictionary describes *a yoke* as follows:

> <u>YOKE</u> - A WOODEN BAR OR FRAME BY WHICH TWO DRAFT ANIMALS (AS OXEN) ARE JOINED AT THE HEADS OR NECKS, WITH THONGS AROUND THEIR NECKS, FOR WORKING TOGETHER. A YOKE OF OXEN IS A PAIR.

Oxen are chosen for their strength and are used for extremely hard work. The yoke has a variety of functions. One of them is to keep both oxen facing in the same direction. Another is to prevent the oxen from looking back. Another is the yoke keeps them joined to work together. The yoke makes the burden lighter by dispersing the load between the two. Yet another is the yoke applies pressure should one of the animals decide to hold back, walk ahead or pull away from the other.

The farmer also helps to guide the animals by using reins. If one animal decides to give up on the job or stops pulling, the yoke will put pressure on him to move. It is then very likely the farmer who oversees the job will prod the animal with a switch to press on. In similar fashion, a man's heart may devise his way, but the Lord directs his steps (Prov. 16:9).

Marriage is a type of yoke. It is a yoke ordained by God. God created woman for man and declared them one, *"and they shall be one flesh"* (Gen. 2:21-24). When you marry, you commit yourself, obligate yourself, give yourself and bind yourself to your husband for care and safekeeping. This yoke or frame that keeps a husband and wife joined together is called *commitment*.

Commitment to your husband and his commitment to you, a covenant you made before Almighty God, is the framework in which each must learn to live in order to find true fulfillment. Marriage commitment is the unseen yoke that ties and links one to the other for the purpose of working together.

The farmer's purpose for his oxen was generally to plow up his field, working systematically from one side to the other. The farmer plans his work and then works his plan. Likewise, the Lord has a purpose for you and your husband. You serve an eternal God with an eternal plan. His purpose is to plow up this world with the gospel of Christ, planting and harvesting. You and your husband are part of His divine plan. He desires to use you and your family to reach the lost. The Lord has entrusted to you a husband and perhaps some children and grandchildren to love, encourage and bless. You need to do all you can to preserve your family and fulfill God's plan while on this lifelong journey.

The farmer uses a pair of oxen attached by a yoke; the Lord also works with a pair. He intends for husband and wife to work together as a team. In fact, if you work together as God intended, it will be as if the farmer were working with only one animal because God sees you as *"one flesh."* Two working together also provide more power and strength for the task.

A husband and wife, living and working together with Jesus as the foundation of their marriage, will be able to withstand anything that comes against them. Yes, the enemy will attack. There will be times when your husband will be weak and will have to rely on your strength. There will be other times when you will be weak and will have to lean on your husband's strength. Together, with faith in Jesus Christ, you will prevail.

"And, if one prevail against him, two shall withstand him; and a threefold cord is not quickly broken," (Eccl. 4:12).

The farmer expects the oxen to stay in line, and he carefully guides the oxen with reins to keep them on the correct path. It is critical to the farmer's plan they do not step out of line. A crooked path could obliterate the farmer's rows, thus spoiling the seeds that were planted and destroying his harvest.

As husbands and wives, we need to encourage, support and help each other to remain on the right and only path leading to heaven. Few find the straight gate and narrow way leading unto life (Matt. 7:14). Don't allow yourself to get diverted. Your way may seem right, but at its end, could be the way of death (Prov. 14:12). God's path will be as a shining light, getting brighter as His Coming draws closer. The way of the wicked will be dark, and the wicked won't even realize what is causing them to stumble (Prov. 4:18-19).

The oxen do not look back. In fact, the yoke they wear around their necks makes it impossible for them to look back. It should be so in a marriage. Your commitment to each other should be strong enough to keep you from dreaming about how your lives might have been better had you remained single. Commitment should prevent you from looking back and wanting something you left behind. Instead, allow the peace of God to settle all questions that arise in your minds (Col. 3:14-15). No man who puts his hand to the plow and looks back is fit for the kingdom of God (Luke 9:62).

A man or woman who marries and continues to wonder about what life would be like single or with someone else is doomed to failure. You need to forget those things which are behind, and strain toward what is ahead. Press on toward the goal to win the prize for which God has called you (Phil. 3:13-14).

Though you may have many past hurts, neither you nor your husband can do one thing to change the past. So bury the past and go on for God. Lay down your hurts at the foot of the Cross.

> *"Remember Lot's wife. Whosoever shall seek to save his life shall lose it; and whosoever shall lose his life shall preserve it,"* (Luke 17:32-33).

She was not willing to forsake the past and walk willingly into an unknown future with her husband. She was the loser and was turned into a pillar of salt (Gen. 19:26).

Should one animal pull away from the other, the pressure put on him by the yoke will cause him pain. Are you experiencing the pressure of your yoke? Have you considered the pressure you feel is there to help you recognize you are pulling away from your husband? Are you stepping away from God's will?

Women's lib has created a horrific number of divorces resulting from women who find it more profitable to live independent of their husbands. Home falls short on their list of priorities as they seek to do their own thing. When pain and pressure strike their homes, these wives quickly leave, end their relationships and break vows once gladly made in the eyes of God. They devalue and reject commitment and show no honor or respect to their husbands. Might we learn something from the animal kingdom? Consider the ox who will automatically pull right back in his proper place to relieve the pain and pressure of his rebellion. Don't keep struggling and fighting for your own way.

When a woman finds herself growing or progressing more rapidly than her husband, beware. She needs to be sensitive to the fact this could very easily add to marital strife if she does not handle things correctly. For instance, when a woman devotes most of her time and energies to a very successful career, this could cause jealousy or resentment in her spouse. Also, when both husband and wife work, quality family time is almost always sacrificed. Your husband will never fight for his place in your life. Only you can honestly answer this question:

Is working outside my home more fulfilling to me than caring for my home and family?

When a woman grows more rapidly in the knowledge of the Word of God, she may drive her husband farther away from the Lord by preaching to him. She calls it *"ministering;"* he calls it *"nagging."* Many wives make the mistake of coming on too strong. Husbands will reject the message when spoken out of frustration, control or super spirituality.

You need to continue to pray for your husband. The Lord will give you opportunities to share with him. When He does, the Holy Spirit will guide you with the words you should speak. He will also show you when to hold your peace.

On a few occasions, I started to respond with an attitude; yet, out of my mouth poured words of kindness instead. I often wondered where those sweet, loving words were coming from. Certainly, the words I was speaking were quite different than the ones I was thinking. Other times, my lips seemed glued together, and I couldn't speak with ease. There were also those times where I felt a check in my spirit and would hold my tongue. What do you think was happening? In answer to my prayers for help, the Holy Spirit was teaching me to control my tongue.

When a woman involves herself in social activities and grows in social graces and her husband is more concerned with comfort than style, you may find a very disgruntled couple. Allow your spouse to be his own man. Be proud of him just the way he is. Growing up wearing dresses and later working in corporate offices, I dressed up all the time. I came home from work and cleaned my house in high heels. My husband's personal preference has always been casual dress. I have learned to enjoy casual dress [even if my casual dress is more on the dressy side]. He has learned there are times to dress up [even if he wears a sport coat with no tie]. I want the freedom to be who I am; and I must allow him the freedom to be the man he chooses to be.

When a woman puts other activities ahead of family and home, this may disrupt the peace in her home. Why? Priorities must have their proper place. Your husband must never lose his place of importance to you. He should never feel he is competing for your love or time.

What if you seem to be progressing faster than your spouse up the various ladders of life--career, social, spiritual, etc.? What if you are becoming increasingly independent? Many women today believe they can do better without their husbands. This will, no doubt, cause heartache and prolong the healing process in your marriage. Remember the oxen. They are joined by a yoke which binds them and keeps them side by side, a team pulling hard to accomplish a mutual goal.

God intends for a married couple to stay yoked together. Since the Lord gave the leadership role to the husband, the wife must learn to come under her husband's authority. This does not mean the Lord loves your husband more than you. He has just given the two of you different functions or roles--the husband is the leader and the wife is the helpmate. When you are both in these roles which were ordained by God, you will be most fulfilled.

If you seem to be growing faster in a particular area, be sure to strongly consider your priorities. It may sound like I am referencing men who are weak or who have problems with insecurity, but I'm not. Your husband may be a remarkably secure individual, a real man's man, yet the enemy can and will use these things to cause division in your marriage. You need to be alert and able to recognize some of the tactics the devil uses to upset the peace in your home. He will use any open door you give him. Guard yourself. You should never trample over your husband, leaving him behind. You should go to extreme measures to include him and love him, while patiently trusting the Lord to work in his heart and life.

The farmer depends on both of the oxen to get the job done, and he does not work with one more than the other. God sees a married couple as *"one flesh."* Therefore, He never calls one without the other, so be assured He is working in both of your lives. Be patient. While waiting on the Lord to work in your husband's heart, the Holy Spirit will be at work in you. He will be perfecting in you love, trust, patience, meekness, chasteness, humility, forbearance, etc. The Lord did not forget about you or store you away on the back of a dusty old shelf somewhere. He knows exactly where you are as well as the conditions you are living in.

One morning in prayer, I cried out to the Lord complaining that the Lord had put me into retirement. No one knew my heart, but I felt useless and without purpose. That very night, in a revival service at a local auditorium, Rev. Jesse Duplantis prayed for me. God really touched me, and Bro. Jesse moved on to the next person in line for prayer. Right before he began praying for that person, he started chuckling and came back to me. He said, "The Lord wanted me to come back and tell you one more thing. You will never retire." We serve such a personal God. He knew my heart that day, and He hears the cries of your heart too.

What happens when an ox refuses to work along with the other? Not only will he experience pain, but the one struggling to work alone will suffer as well. It will be much harder on the one trying to carry the load of two. If the pressure of the yoke is not enough to pull the ox back in line, the farmer will prod the animal with a switch if necessary. Will the Lord have to prod you with a switch? He wants your marriage whole, and God will chasten those He loves (Rev. 3:19).

Also, if the yoke of oxen refuses to work together, the farmer will eventually have to replace it. The Lord has a plan and purpose for you and your husband, and He wants to use you as a team. However, there are times you and your husband may miss opportunities intended for the two of you. Instead, God may give those opportunities to another team to accomplish His purpose. Do not give up on the union God has joined together.

> *"Yet ye say, Wherefore? Because the Lord hath been witness between thee and the wife of thy youth; against whom thou hast dealt treacherously: yet is she thy companion, and the wife of thy covenant. And did not he make one? Yet had he the residue of the spirit. And wherefore one? That he might seek a godly seed. Therefore take heed to your spirit, and let none deal treacherously against the wife of his youth. For the Lord, the God of Israel saith that he hateth putting away…" (Mal. 2:14-16).*

The Lord has witnessed this marriage in Malachi, and He has not missed the fact that this husband has dealt treacherously against the wife of his youth. You and your husband were joined by a blood covenant which was witnessed by God. In the Scripture above, it is very clear this husband has not been the perfect husband; however, *"the Lord, the God of Israel, says he hates putting away,"* [divorce].

In Mark, Chapter 10, the Pharisees came to Jesus questioning whether it was lawful for a man to divorce his wife. They were tempting Him. He answered with a question, *"What did Moses command you?"* They told Him Moses said they could write a bill of divorcement and put her away. Listen to what Jesus said to them:

> *"And Jesus answered and said unto them, For the hardness of your heart he wrote you this precept. But from the beginning of the creation God made them male and female. For this cause shall a man leave his father and mother, and cleave to his wife; And they twain shall be one flesh: so then they are no more twain, but one flesh. What therefore God hath joined together, let not man put asunder." (Mark 10:5-9).*

They continued to push the issue, and they asked Him again. Isn't it interesting how people back then, even those in the church, sought His approval to divorce? He answered:

> *"Whosoever shall put away his wife, and marry another, committeth adultery against her. And if a woman shall put away her husband, and be married to another, she committeth adultery,"* (Mark 10:11-12).

Notice that Jesus said Moses wrote this precept regarding a bill of divorcement because of the *hardness of their hearts*. Might hardness of hearts be the main cause of divorce today? God will work with you to save your marriage. Realize that no husband is impossible for God. No marriage is impossible for God. No situation in your life is impossible for God. Continue to pray against the principalities and spirits that have your husband bound. Knowing that God hates divorce, how much more do you think He will work with you to heal your marriage and save your husband? Let me encourage you, even in the worst situations, God is still on the throne.

> *"What shall we then say to these things? If God be for us, who can be against us, "* (Rom. 8:31)?

As you reflect on your wedding day, both you and your husband made a vow in the presence of God which was witnessed by many other family members and friends. You were happy and excited to make that vow. When you spoke those words, you meant them with all your heart.

> *"When thou vowest a vow unto God, defer not to pay it; for he hath no pleasure in fools; pay that which thou hast vowed. Better is it that thou shouldest not vow, than that thou shouldest vow and not pay,"* (Eccl. 5:4-5).

The Lord expects you to do your part in keeping your vows. Don't devour what is holy by questioning after making a vow to Him (Prov. 20:25). Don't try to defend yourself by telling God it was all a mistake. I have heard Christian women attempt to justify divorce by believing they vowed in marriage to the wrong man. In their hearts, they are really hoping God's forgiveness for their choices will include His approval of divorce. They believe they are doomed to suffer their entire lives for making poor choices. They believe God will never use them in the work of His kingdom. Some have even bought into the lie they are being punished with unhappiness for making wrong choices. These are lies from the pit of hell. The devil would love nothing more than to keep you dreaming of how your life might have been better if only you had waited for another, or God's choice. The Lord knows and sees where you are. Even if your marriage was the direct result of disobedience, there is forgiveness and healing available for you. He does not expect you to bail out of your marriage and break up your home and family for you to find your special guy. You need to press forward with the Lord. Begin where you are right now and intercede for the salvation of your husband. God is perfectly able to redeem your marriage, turning your poor choice into the perfect choice.

Years ago, I prayed at the altar with a very distraught woman who had been living a hopeless life because she believed this lie. She had met her husband at a club. She had been raised in a Christian home, rebelled as a teenager and ended up pregnant. She lived in terrifying fear God would punish her by taking her baby. She believed the lie that she deserved a life of punishment and somehow God was going to "get her." She felt her bad marriage was what she deserved and something she must accept. If this is true, then Jesus died in vain. She missed God's whole purpose for giving His only Son on the Cross at Calvary.

Have you already suffered a divorce? Are you now struggling in your second or third marriage? The Lord will meet you right where you are, regardless of what number husband he is--even number four, five or six. Certainly, you cannot go back and try to fix your past. Yesterday is gone. Give Him your past. Jesus wants to meet you *today*.

It is important I make this crystal clear. There was a false prophet who came to Chalmette, Louisiana, many years ago. A middle-aged lady went up for prayer at one of his meetings held at a local auditorium. Her heart was open to God and sincere before Him. She was divorced from her first husband and had remarried. She had been happily married for ten years to her second husband and had three beautiful children. This false prophet told her she was living in sin. He instructed her to divorce her second husband who was also the father of her three children and return to her first love. This is hogwash. This false prophet was being used by the devil to destroy this woman and her family. By the time she walked into our church office seeking pastoral advice, she was frantic and confused.

We cannot go back and untangle the webs we made of our lives. However, when we meet Jesus, it is a new day. He receives us where we are--married, single, remarried, divorced or widowed. He meets us at our point of need, and He takes us to greater heights than we've ever dreamed.

No doubt, marital stress hurts. The pain you feel is real. Instead of considering this pain as a sign your marriage is over, won't you consider it a sign your marriage needs work? You are not at the end of the road. Help is in sight. The realization your marriage needs help gives the Lord an opportunity to work a miracle in your home. Joining God's plan and His desire for your marriage to be successful gives you all the power and wisdom you will need to succeed. "Not giving up" is a choice only you can make. Join God's team. Work with Him--not against Him--to save your marriage.

The Lord might be saying some things to you that seem hard. He may be speaking words to you that make you wince--words you don't want to hear. He may be telling you something similar to what He told me many years ago:

"My daughter, quit looking at circumstances. Get in line with my Word. Be the wife and mother I want you to be. Center your attention on me. Trust your husband to me. Follow me and stop doing things your way."

God wants you to be linked with your husband to work with him and lighten his load. Pull with your husband in the same direction. Quit trying to play tug-of-war. It is not God's will at all for two people to be married and live two independent lives, each struggling for his own way. In Christ, there is so much more available to you. The Lord wants you to experience closeness and an intimacy as "one flesh."

A man must love his wife as he loves himself; and a wife must see to it that she deeply respects her husband--obeying, praising and honoring him (Eph. 5:33). You may be thinking it is impossible to praise, honor or respect your husband. He has not loved you as himself. Neither has he loved you as Christ loves the church. Therefore, you have alleged that until he does his part, you are not responsible for your part.

This might be what is called "tough" love, but God has not exempted you from obedience to His Word. Regardless of how much you feel your husband doesn't deserve your respect, your obedience will release the Lord to work on your behalf and in your husband's life. Your obedience will remove barriers. It will remove opportunities for your husband to justify his ungodly behavior by blaming you or responding to you with angry retaliation. Instead, he will see himself as he is, a sinner needing a Savior.

Do you realize marriage is a privilege? God has given you a special privilege and honor to be married and share in your beloved's life and dreams. Your husband did not have to choose you to be his life-long mate, but he did. Remember the day he proposed to you. You couldn't wait to be part of his life. You would go anywhere and do anything just to be with him. Now that you are married, must he drag you along like an anchor chained to his ankle in order to accomplish his dreams? When you are truly one, his dreams will become your dreams.

Support him and encourage him to reach his goals. It is important that you have discussions with him and establish common goals to work toward together. Your husband should never have to fit into your mold. You should be living your life in such a way that his will, his dreams and his goals are also yours as you *adapt* to your own husband as a service to the Lord (Eph. 5:22). Use every talent and ability God has given you to complete him and make his dreams come true. In doing so, you will find fulfillment. Comfort him, encourage him and commit yourself to doing him only good for as long as you live (Prov. 31:12).

Your husband will be more willing to reciprocate unselfish love by helping you, spending quality time with you, and by preferring you and the things you enjoy. He will no longer be forced to fight for the leadership of his home. With the element of competition removed, he will be free to show you love and respect, appreciating God's blessings in you and through you, such as skills, intellect, talent and wisdom.

If you know your marriage is not where it needs to be, you must admit your marriage needs help. Accept the fact your marriage needs work. Let this be the igniter that causes you to begin working to make your home a happier place. Sometimes, we have only one desire, to place blame or point the finger. Where is your finger pointing? Do any of these sound familiar?

- "Lord, if only he would get saved."
- "Lord, if only he would be my spiritual leader."
- "Lord, if only he would put me first."
- "Lord, if only he would spend more time with me and the kids."
- "Lord, if only you would change my husband."

Put these thoughts right out of your mind. I exhausted myself with years of praying for the Lord to change my husband, only to find He was more concerned with changing me. Concentrate on what God expects of you, not what you expect of your husband. You can only control your own actions and your own choices. The changes you make can then positively affect another's, (i.e. your spouse's actions).

This should be a prayer from your heart:

> "Lord, change me, and make me into the woman you want me to be. Help me to please You. Lord, help me to die to self."

When you live in obedience to God's Word, the Lord honors your prayers. He will not honor the prayers of a rebellious wife. He will not honor the prayers of a rebellious heart. Allow the Lord to change you. Conform to His will and you will be a blessed woman.

The Lord knows your husband's heart, and He knows exactly what it will take to reach him. The Lord will lead him to that place if you will only let Him.

The Word of God teaches a woman's actions are more profitable in ministering to her husband than the words she speaks. In other words, she is more likely to reach her husband when she is "walking the walk" and not just "talking the talk." Let your husband see and experience Jesus' love through you.

Many women fear being "walked on" by their husbands. They fear becoming "doormats." Both are phrases we hear way too often. Yes, abuse has created a lack of trust. Yes, women have been wounded by the men they love. Sadly, women who use these phrases most, more often than not, want everything their way. They lack real understanding of the victory God can bring to a submitted life. They indisputably refuse to apply God's Word to their lives.

Allow God's Word to get into your spirit. Put your total trust in the Lord. You will be amazed at how God will move in your home with indescribable power. Everything that can be shaken will be shaken. Get ready.

Consider the following Scripture. Read it over and over until you believe it.

> *"Likewise, ye wives, be in subjection to your own husbands; that if any obey not the word, they also may without the word be won by the conversation of the wives; While they behold your chaste conversation coupled with fear. Whose adorning let it not be that outward adorning of plaiting the hair, and of wearing of gold, or of putting on of apparel; But let it be the hidden man of the heart, in that which is not corruptible, even the ornament of a meek and quiet spirit, which is in the sight of God of great price. For after this manner in the old time the holy women also, who trusted in God, adorned themselves, being in subjection unto their own husbands; Even as Sara obeyed Abraham, calling him lord; whose daughters ye are, as long as ye do well, and are not afraid with any amazement," (1 Pet. 3:1-6).*

Don't be controlled by the spirit of fear. Giving way to fear will completely immobilize you, preventing you from taking any positive steps toward saving your marriage.

In my own life, there was one lesson I practiced that helped me conquer fear. Every time fear tempted me to pull away or back away, I would purpose in my heart to do the exact opposite. I would press in that much more. Therefore, the devil could not control me with fear. As you submit to God and resist the devil, the devil will flee.

My husband had been planning for us to go to a party. He talked about the party all week. Fear began gripping my heart and I wanted to pull away. I no longer wanted to be part of that world. I wanted to come out and be separate. I knew the party would include things I wanted out of my life. Had I refused to go, it would have caused a major argument. He would have received my outright refusal to go as my personal rejection of him. My dilemma was this was not the message I wanted to send him.

The Lord had been teaching me to take my needs to Him first and trust Him. I continued taking that party before the Lord in prayer. I genuinely believed and trusted the Lord as I submitted my husband's request before God. With my trust in God and not in man, I was then able to press in, showering my husband with love and acceptance. You see, my flesh wanted to knock him over the head with a frying pan for desiring to hang onto the world. I wanted to correct. I wanted to lead. The Lord helped me to do the opposite. I was confident the Lord would make a way of escape for me. I knew fighting and arguing wasn't the answer. Refusing to go in the name of Christianity would not help draw him to the Lord either. Believing in faith, I continued to place my need before God in prayer.

The party was Friday night. Friday morning, my husband left for work still planning to go to the party. No doubt, at this point, my faith was being tested. Friday, at 4:30 p.m., my husband called from work. There had been a problem at the office, and he was forced to work until 6:30 p.m., running him too late to come home and then return to downtown New Orleans in time for the party. I could hear the disappointment in his voice as he apologized for not being able to take me to the party of the year. Instead, he came home and we went out for a quiet, romantic dinner.

Don't you know I was shouting on the inside? Can you see God's hand in this last-minute change of plans? The Lord had intervened. I had put my faith and trust in Him, and He had answered my prayers. He made a way of escape for me, and my husband did not realize God was involved in causing him to work overtime that evening. The Lord came through right on time. Thankfully, He is never late. Don't lose faith. He will not be late for you either.

The Word of God also teaches the principle of sowing and reaping. If you want a friend, show yourself friendly. If you want kindness, sow kindness. If you want love, sow love. If you want forgiveness, you must be willing to forgive. If you want mercy, sow mercy. This principle may be applied to any need in our lives. It works. God will use you in a mighty way to restore and repair your home. You must commit yourself to your marriage. If you want a committed husband, then *first* be a committed wife. Pour your love into your husband and bless his life.

It is easy to be obligated and committed to the one you love. When you truly love your husband, it is also a light burden to serve him and be subject to him. Therefore, God has given you a mission if you should decide to accept it. The two of you were yoked together and chosen for a purpose. You have a destiny to fulfill together. Go the extra mile. Make the choice to love your husband unconditionally.

If you want to be blessed, then first do everything within your power to be a blessing. Attempt to give him your very best in love and deed. The Lord receives everything you do for your husband as if you were doing it unto Him. Keeping this mindset will strengthen your faith. Your determination will please the Lord.

Even during those times when love may not be immediately reciprocated, you will have the assurance that God is blessed by your obedience to His Word. Eventually, by consistently pouring out unconditional love, you will turn your husband's head and win his favor. Don't give up. Love melts the hardest of hearts.

> *"...ye are thereunto called, that ye should inherit a blessing!" (1 Pet 3:8-9).*

LORD, HEAL OUR MARRIAGE

CHAPTER NINE
OUCH! DYING HURTS!

In our marriages, there are times when everything is going great; everyone seems happy; finances are good; and our marital relationships seem to be everything we could possibly desire. Then suddenly something happens that turns our lives upside down. Things that appear secure can quickly change overnight.

One such time in my marriage was the day my husband asked me to quit my job to become a full-time mother to our children. For many women, this would have been an answer to prayer. At the time, this seemed to me to be a very selfish request. Let me explain.

I had worked outside the home for years and easily fell into a career pattern. I had worked my way from the mail room to my new position as Section Chief, and had excelled in the workplace. A change in my new duties required travel, and I was not leaving my new baby. Wanting to stay at home with my first baby, I gave a three-month notice and resigned. This resignation was of my own choosing. This was the first time in my married life I had been a full-time homemaker. Excellence was always important to me, and I quickly found that I was not proficient at many things stay-at-home church moms seemed to enjoy like sewing, quilting, crafts or book clubs. I hated housework and ironing, and I did not know how to cook. Homemaking was boring and unfulfilling to me. I had very little common ground to share when in a group of moms, and I didn't enjoy those times. I had very little tolerance for the conversations I often heard, i.e. whining, complaining, gossip, etc. Spending time with my handsome baby boy was my one reward for being a stay-at-home mom. My focus was entirely on him.

As soon as our son grew old enough, I was asked to help out in the church office. I began working part-time at the church and Christian school when needed. When he became school age, I found myself back at work full-time at our church. Working only during school hours brought me much satisfaction. I enjoyed it. I loved administration and was gifted with organizational skills. I was recognized often for doing an exceptional job and thrived on the challenges put before me. On the job, my creativity flourished. Once again, I postponed any improvements in the homemaking department.

When my son was five, we were blessed with a beautiful baby girl. I took a leave of absence. When my daughter was a few months old, I had to make a decision. Once again, I tried the balancing act. I knew how worthless I felt being at home all the time. I reasoned that if I only worked part-time, even if just a few days, I could handle both. My oldest was now in school. A friend offered to keep my baby, and she lived within a block of the church. I went back to work and limited my schedule to only two days per week, school hours only. I convinced myself that two days would help the church and get me out of the house too. Even so, I operated on a very rigid schedule to accomplish everything required of a working mom. I spent many late nights trying to play catch-up around the house. The workload had picked up at the church. It was obvious that a few days could easily turn into more very soon.

Early one morning, sitting on the sofa in the den and enjoying my first cup of coffee, my husband's words jolted me awake. He said, "Pam, if you love me, I want you to stay at home and raise our children. I chose you to be the mother of my children. I want them to learn from you, not their sitter." I found out later two incidents had prompted this request. One day, he heard our baby babbling "Ma Ma Ma Ma Ma Ma" to our babysitter. The incident that clinched it was finding his baby girl, still a little wobbly sitting up, splashing with the babysitter's child in a wading pool in the front yard of the babysitter's house. Her house was on a very busy street, and the babysitter was inside watching through the window [she really was watching]. No doubt, she should have been outside with the children. That day, he snatched his baby girl up and came home knowing she would never go back.

Needless to say, his words penetrated deep, reaching the innermost part of my heart and piercing my soul. I was at a loss for words. My slow and defensive reply was, "How can you begin to question my love for you and our children?" The truth is I loved them very much. Since he traveled, I was the one who devoted more time to the training of our children. Finances were also tight, and I thought I was helping out. We had put our son in private school. I had justified it in my own mind that my husband needed me to work.

The Holy Spirit was at work though and quickly brought to mind when Jesus asked Peter, *"lovest thou me?"* Peter loved the Lord with all his heart; he followed Him wherever He went; he wanted to be part of His ministry; he wanted to learn from Him; and he wanted to be His friend. Jesus wanted more from Peter when He said to him, *"feed my sheep"* (John 21:15-17). To carry out this assignment, Peter was going to have to forsake all and die to self. He would need to give up any ambitions he may have had for himself to obey and follow the Lord. Jesus wanted a self-sacrificing love from Peter. I realized that long-ago day my husband was looking for a self-sacrificing love from me. It hurt me to realize I had never been fully able to give that kind of love.

This was not an unreasonable request for him to make of me. In fact, he wanted me home because he loved me. He saw the strain and pressure that goes with being a working mother. He didn't say I had become slack in my duties. In fact, he often praised me for doing both well. However, at times, he saw me tired and pushing hard to keep up with both work and home. He really wanted more of my time, and I did not realize his wishes then. He loved me enough that he wanted our children growing up with my habits, my training and my love. He even prayed our little girl would grow up to be an exact duplicate of me.

His request, however, was a difficult one. Office work was the only thing I knew how to do well. I had trained all through high school and developed many clerical skills. I excelled in office administration since I began working in corporate offices at only seventeen years of age (with a certificate from the St. Bernard School Board). I continued to question, "Am I really doing wrong by working only two days per week?"

The real truth was that I feared being a homemaker. I had never learned how. As a homemaker, I was a square peg trying to fit into a round hole. I seemed out of place in this setting and feared being a failure. I felt worthless. I was horrible in the kitchen, and everything I cooked tasted terrible. I felt I could not serve the Lord at home. Or, could I? Although I wouldn't admit it, I knew the Lord was stretching me. He was teaching me how to love.

God's love *gives* at the expense of self. If things must go your way, you are not walking in God's love. God's love always gives. It always prefers another. The opposite of love would be lust which *takes* to please one's self at the expense of others.

My husband helped me to see that I was needed at home. I loved my children. They were everything to me. I didn't want to fail them in any way. In obedience, I once again laid down my job and ministry to be a homemaker. I knew our finances would be crunched, and I would have no extra spending money. I also knew God's Word instructed me to obey and submit to my husband's authority (1 Pet. 3:1). With a deliberate act of obedience, I resigned. I did my best not to complain, and I began conquering the task of learning how to be a better homemaker, wife and mother. Up to this point in my life, much of my efforts had been directed outside the home. It was what this career-minded woman knew best. I had devoted little concentrated effort to learning homemaking skills. God had a plan. He wanted me to fulfill my God-given role by creating a loving, warm environment that my family could call home. The Lord was continuing to form me into His image.

At first, there was a major problem with me being home. I had way too much idle time as compared to my past daily work schedule. The enemy began setting up a workshop in my mind. With the enemy whispering in my ears regularly, I began ruminating past hurts. I began questioning the true condition of my husband's heart. Was he really leading me to do the right thing? Was it what God wanted or was the devil using him to destroy my effectiveness in ministry? I continued to silently question his motives. Was he really looking out for me and the children, or was he scheming to give himself more free time to do what he wanted to do? Fear would creep in as I allowed myself to entertain thoughts that were not of God. I was plagued with *"what-if-I-tis."*

Finally, realizing my fearful condition, I determined in my heart to do the opposite. Time would bring to light the truth. In the meantime, I knew I needed to trust God and love my husband. Thankfully, God did know my husband's heart. His decision was based on what he thought was best for our family. He felt I would be more fulfilled as a woman. He knew my children needed me. What he didn't realize at the time was how much he needed me too. Surprisingly, in time, I even learned how to cook. That's a real miracle.

God began blessing me in many ways, confirming to my heart that He knew where I was and what I was going through. He let me know He would help me through all of the adjustments that were slapping me squarely in the face as a result of this transition. Little by little, I realized my greatest ministry had been at home all the time--ministering to my family.

Eventually, I settled into a workable routine. My time each day with the Lord became more and more precious to me too. He probably had been trying to talk to me for a long time. Now, I was listening. Isn't it true we can get too busy to hear from God? When I prayed, I did not always take the time to listen for the Lord's voice. My mind was cluttered with tomorrow's agenda and appointments, and I failed to notice when the Lord was speaking to me. After I was home, my life really slowed down. I recognized that God was dealing with me and I was ready to hear every word He had to say. He took me through a training program one step and one day at a time. I almost felt like He was creating me all over again. I'm sure He was. He was definitely renewing my mind.

From the perspective of hindsight, I thank the Lord each day for a husband who gave this wife the opportunity to invest in our children. They have both grown into responsible adults who love the Lord. They continue to bring honor to us, and we are proud of them and their beautiful families. The world had me convinced my career determined my value. I was deceived. Actually, the opposite is true. It is impossible to put a value on a godly mother. They are priceless and no job gives one a greater return on their investment.

It did not take me long to realize I was the one who had been motivated by selfishness. It was not that I did not love my husband or children--they were my life. I poured myself into my children and into my home, giving them all I had to invest. Like many career-minded individuals, though, I had bought into the lie that homemakers were ignorant and useless, with nothing "to bring to the table." The secular world does not recognize value in homemakers or stay-at-home moms. Therefore, I juggled family and work trying to find the perfect balance. Just for the record, for me, there was no perfect balance. No matter how efficient I was, or how hard I worked to balance my time or how many extra hours I worked, something always fell short. Unfortunately, it was my family that fell short most of the time. Any mother trying to balance both work and family will experience pressure from all sides.

I know that not every mom has the luxury of being a stay-at-home mom. Some must work outside of the home.

Many single moms must also support their families. For those of you who work outside the home, you will have to work much harder. It is possible to give your family its rightful place on your list of priorities. Some of your greatest blessings will come from the sacrificial love you give them.

Perchance, it's not a job that is causing you undue stress. It may be hobbies, pleasures, church involvement or demands from other family members. It might be something else entirely. Your time can be robbed by anything you put ahead of God, your husband and your children.

You may mistakenly consider it a supreme sacrifice when you begin to put your family first under God and strive to realign your priorities. To the contrary, you will be on the receiving end of some of the greatest blessings you will ever receive. God notices as you struggle with the change. He sees your obedience as unto Him, and His blessings will follow. There is no question the Lord has abundantly blessed our family. His blessings began the day I obeyed my husband, laid down my independence and gave my family its rightful priority.

Norman Miller, Pasadena School Psychologist, in an interview by Donna Scheibe of the *Los Angeles Times* lays out some interesting thoughts on the subject of *"feminine dependency."*

> *"When a woman tells me she has to have a career or must work outside the home because she would go stark raving mad as just a housewife, then I know she doesn't want to be an equal side of a triangle. She wants to be the main rod in a geometric arrangement where the father or children have less stature. Mothers who come to school counselors or psychologists when their children are in trouble give many reasons for working outside the home. Some are valid, but many are not. They'll tell you their husbands just don't take*

hold. (I'm assuming she means they will not take the lead.) The painful part is that any husband is head of any home only as long as his wife holds him in that capacity--only as long as her side of the triangle is a firmly welded support. You have to give your husband the lead and let him fumble with it, and realize that he'll fumble many times. It is a man who must succeed outside the home. Woman's greatest satisfactions are found within it. Only there is she really irreplaceable. The mother is not only the main prop of her husband in holding the triangle firm, but she must weld her children into their supportive position. The mother who uses her femininity, her intuitiveness, her warmth of spirit to the absolute ultimate, plays a large part in molding the respect a child has for his father's masculinity. And this a child must absolutely have. It's vital for a boy to identify with his father. He must be comfortable in identifying as a male, and a girl child must be aware of her father's maleness even as she wants to be like her mother. Children must know that their parents are two different kinds of people and that father and mother respect this."

When both of my children were school age, I was then able to work part-time around the children's schedule--this time with my husband's blessing. By then, God had done a major work in my heart, and priorities were in order.

"And they all lived happily ever after..." Not. Just when I'd become very well adjusted and comfortable, God tapped me on the shoulder, disturbing my comfort zone. My husband wanted to move to Mississippi. He was raised in Mobile, Alabama, loved country life, and wanted to get away from the faster-paced suburban lifestyle. A commute to New Orleans only once per week would keep his daily work routine about the same. For me, although I had verbally agreed to the move, I would be leaving my job, my church, my prayer partners, my friends and our family. In other words, I would be leaving my entire support system.

I knew he was excited about the possibility, so I gave the idea to the Lord. We had tried selling our house a few years earlier when his New Orleans office moved to Baton Rouge. It did not sell, and he was forced to change governmental agencies which brought his office back to New Orleans. This setback in selling our home increased my confidence the Lord would not allow us to move if it was not His will for us. I was, therefore, able to get excited with my husband.

To my husband's surprise and my shock, two weeks after putting our "For Sale" sign out, an 80 year-old woman walked into our home and offered us cash. Our Chalmette home was sold with no firm plans in place as to where we were moving.

To make a long story short, the Lord worked everything out for us quickly and we moved to McNeil, Mississippi. Our new home was a beautiful cedar house in the midst of eight landscaped acres. This garden-like setting made us feel as if we had gone on a retreat, and God had given us this retreat center as our home. It reminded me of a mini Bellingrath Gardens, though not nearly as elaborately landscaped. It was peaceful and picturesque and sat in the center of majestic oaks. It was filled with all types of birds, rabbits, squirrels and other wildlife. The beautiful grounds were fragrant with hundreds of blooming azaleas, lilies, gardenias, daffodils, wisteria, honeysuckle and sweet olive. It was a dream-come-true place for us.

I had put my trust in the Lord, and I seemed to be content with our decision to move to this lovely place. At least, I thought I could handle it. We said our last goodbyes to family and friends and settled into our new home.

I'm sorry to admit, after two years had passed, I was still rubbing the bark off my juniper tree and whining like Elijah

(1 King 19:4). I complained and moaned about the adjustments I had to make from city to country life. I was miserable, and I made everyone around me miserable. The frustration grew until one day I packed my bags and announced I was moving back home [meaning Louisiana] with my children.

The Lord began dealing with my heart after I upset our entire household. I repented and gave up. I surrendered. I decided to be content in whatever "State" I was in, and my attitude began to change. Joy came back into our home.

In Mississippi, my charming son graduated valedictorian from high school and college and has since become a physician in family medicine. He met my precious daughter-in-law at our Mississippi church. Within the past ten years, they have blessed us with five beautiful grandchildren. In Mississippi, my dazzling daughter graduated from high school and college with honors; she married a sharp young man, now an intellectual properties lawyer, who was also from our Mississippi church. In the past ten years, they have blessed us with four adorable grandchildren.

In Mississippi, my husband was able to work from our home up until he retired in 2007. He enjoyed looking out of his office windows at the beautiful countryside where wild deer and turkey occasionally played in our yard. Our togetherness in a more isolated setting created an atmosphere that allowed a close bond to develop in our family--and love grew. My husband blessed me with my dream home where we enjoyed many gatherings with family and friends. Blessings rained upon our family in Mississippi. Many of our most treasured family memories with our children took place in Mississippi.

I was unable to see the future, but the Lord had a plan for our lives. Rebelling to the move would have caused me to miss out on many happy years with my husband and children.

The Lord will lead your family by directing it through the priest and head of your home, your husband. As you follow that plan in obedience, the atmosphere of your home will begin to change. Having a heart free of rebellion will give you a greater confidence and trust in the Lord. Yes, dying hurts. Yes, you will feel your flesh rising up when you hear the word "no." Yes, your flesh will scream when you don't get your way. However, your obedience is the key that will unlock the windows of heaven for God's blessings to pour upon your home and family.

Never would I have guessed moving to Mississippi might have been preparation for future moves to come in later years. Contract jobs since retirement have taken us to various places where we have been privileged to meet wonderful new friends and see many beautiful places. When, where and how God opened the doors, we went. Somehow, along the way, God must have worked into me the ability to be flexible or this would never have been possible. I've learned to be content in whatever "State" I am in. I have learned to adapt and go with the flow, enjoying the journey along the way. I have been willing to follow my husband's lead. An added benefit has been that the quality time we have enjoyed together as a couple has been irreplaceable. This is definitely the result of God supernaturally transforming my heart and life.

After four years of working in various states and living out of hotel suites, small apartments or condos, we once again put down roots. Our new home is now located on a bluff, giving us a winter view of beautiful Lake Guntersville. The setting of our Alabama home is private, peaceful and wooded where we often see deer in our yard. John, once again, has been blessed to work out of a home office, where he enjoys viewing the wildlife from his office windows.

Through the years, we heard others say there is nothing like grandchildren. How true! The Lord has filled our lives with multiple blessings, nine beautiful grandchildren, our oldest being only eight years-old. These children are the joy of our lives, and we love them beyond measure. With a heart filled with gratitude, we thank the Lord each day for the one blessing closest to our hearts--our family. Our loving family is amazing. It is the greatest.

Hopefully, by now, you can see why I am such a strong believer in God's restoration power. Dying to self and giving God the reins was the catapult to these blessings in my life. I serve a miracle-working God. His best is just ahead for you, too. Give Him the reins. Allow Him to fill your life with His goodness and lead you to the purpose He has planned for you and your family.

CHAPTER TEN
BUT, YOU DON'T KNOW MY HUSBAND!

King Ahaseurus, king of Persia, held a feast for 180 days. This was the longest feast on record. Being filled with vanity, the king wanted to show off the riches of his kingdom and the honor of his majesty. The 180 days of feasting ended with a seven-day feast for all the people. The Book of Esther reveals King Ahaseurus was merry with wine on the seventh day of this seven-day feast. As a result of his egotism and drunkenness, He sent his chamberlains to bring Queen Vashti before him in royal apparel to show off her beauty to the princes and people.

The queen refused. She had good reason. It was an unusual demand for the king to bring her before drunken revelers. His demand did not show respect for her modesty, dignity or rank as queen. According to Persian custom, the queen was not to uncover her eyes nor was she to appear in public. Obeying his request would expose her to common people. Furthermore, it was normally the custom for the king to summon the queen by sending his nobles. This time, he sent his chamberlains or household servants instead. She very likely was keenly aware her husband would never have made such a request or tolerated such exposure had he been sober. Wasn't his honor also at stake? Her trust in her husband's ability to lead and her confidence in his ability to make wise choices were no doubt shaken. Nevertheless, queens and concubines of kings were subject to the complete will of monarchs, the same as slaves. Her disobedience humiliated the king before his subjects, and he became very angry.

Instead of obeying her husband's request and allowing him to face the subsequent consequences, she did what many women do when they feel their husbands are making a mistake. She usurped his authority. Possibly, she did this to protect him from the disgrace his actions would cause. Let's give her the benefit of the doubt. Her motive may have been to protect his honor. Nevertheless, she took over the leadership role and dishonored the king's position by refusing his request. She may have had good reasons, but reasons alone were not enough. She still publicly rebelled and disobeyed her husband and king.

What did she gain by her rebellious actions? Did the king appreciate her response? No, he did not. She gained no favor with her husband. Her disobedience challenged his ability to rule his own house and kingdom. She publicly set a bad example for the other women, and the men feared that their wives would follow her rebellious example. Her disobedience cost her everything. She lost the respect and favor of her husband, her home, all that was rightfully hers and her royal position as queen. Another would now take her place.

Queen Vashti faced the hard reality that God cannot and will not add His blessings to disobedience and rebellion. *"To obey is better than sacrifice"* (1 Sam. 15:22), and *"rebellion is as the sin of witchcraft"* (1 Sam. 15:23). This lesson teaches us the importance of making wise and obedient choices.

You may think this is terribly unfair. After all, Queen Vashti had "rights," didn't she? You may ask, "Don't I have rights?" When challenged with obedience, you may be provoked to cry out, "But, you don't know my husband!"

It is true you may be one of many who live in very difficult marriages. I am not minimizing the grief or hardship you bear. It's also true I may not know your husband. However, one thing is unquestionably clear. Queen Esther knew Queen Vashti's husband. They both married the same man; yet, Queen Esther had better results. Let's learn from the better example.

As a virgin maiden, Queen Esther had gone through the one-year purification process to prepare herself for her king. She purified herself six months with oil of myrrh and six months with sweet odors and with other things for the purifying of the women. She was simple but beautiful. She obtained favor and grace in the king's sight and the king made her queen instead of Queen Vashti. Take note that Esther prepared herself *physically* for her king.

During the day, my mom worked extremely hard, but she always stopped in the evenings and prepared herself for my dad's arrival home from work. She always made sure she was bathed, smelling sweet and looking her best for her king. She always had something ready to serve him, hot coffee in the winter and iced tea or lemonade in the hot summer. Dinner was prepared and ready. She always set his place at the head of the table showing him honor and respect. She made sure that his castle was clean and orderly. The children were already bathed and dressed for daddy's arrival home as well. Why? The king was coming home, and her excitement and joy in anticipation of his arrival became contagious. She treated him like a king, and he loved and enjoyed all of her pampering. What an example she set for her daughters and granddaughters.

As a woman, you know true beauty goes much deeper than the outward appearance. You also know the Lord looks upon our hearts. Though both of these thoughts are 100 percent true, they often become excuses. Let me explain. Many wives do not take the care of their physical appearances seriously after marriage. For some, it is as if saying, "I do" removes their need to prepare themselves for their husbands. You would be surprised at the number of husbands who go home in the evenings to wives who have not yet dressed for the day, fixed their hair, brushed their teeth or even bathed, much less made any attempt to look their best for them. Many complaints came through our church office by husbands for this very reason.

These complaints really surprised me. Sadly, these wives are forgetting one very important point. They are dangerously ignoring the fact men do notice the outward appearance (1 Sam. 16:7). Ladies, your husbands may appreciate inner beauty. They may thank the Lord each day you have a heart after God. These will not replace the fact that they will notice outward appearance. God created them that way. Don't you want them to be noticing you, rather than looking elsewhere?

Do you remember when you were dating your husband? If he was coming to visit, you would shower, shave your legs, fix your hair and makeup, paint your nails, and apply lotion and perfume. You made sure you looked and smelled your absolute best for his arrival. You need to maintain that same excitement and anticipation of being with your mate. Regardless of how many years you have been married, take a few minutes each day to prepare yourself physically for your husband. Do the most with what God gave you. Give your husband your best, whatever your best is. He will notice your outward appearance. That's a promise.

Queen Esther was faced with a difficult problem. She had received word her people would be killed, and she needed to make an appeal to the king. She was not to go before the king unless the king called for her and held out his golden scepter or she could be put to death. This was law.

Queen Esther's motive was to help others, and she was willing to put her life on the line. She asked that her people join her in prayer and fasting for three days. It is impressive that Queen Esther's very first step when faced with a problem was taking her need to the Lord in prayer. Together, Esther and her people hoped prayer and fasting would move the heart of God and He would touch the heart of the king to spare them. Unlike Queen Vashti's rebellious influence, Queen Esther's submissive influence turned others toward God. Do you see she prepared herself *spiritually* for her king with prayer and fasting? She knew the king's heart was in the hand of the Lord, and He could turn it whithersoever He willed (Prov. 21:1).

On the third day, Queen Esther stood in the inner room over against the king's house where the king could see her from his royal throne, but she did not approach him. She waited patiently for the king to hold out his golden scepter to receive her and he did. It is important to note that Queen Esther, even under duress with lives at stake, did not disrespectfully disobey her king. She did not burst into the inner room, run straight to his throne and immediately pour all her problems out on the king. Instead, she submitted her problem to the Lord, trusted Him and proceeded slowly, not desiring to displease her king. This shows a *submissive spirit*.

The story goes on to say she prepared banquet meals for him, *serving and honoring* him, eventually making her request known to her king. She was patient and she waited. The king showed her favor.

Sometimes, you may want to request something of your husband which may be a difficult or uncomfortable request. Perhaps your husband is not a Christian. How should you handle inviting him to a revival service or to a Christmas drama at your local church? The key lies in your approach. Learn from Queen Esther's example.

- *Prepare spiritually* for your husband by seeking the Lord with prayer and fasting. Seek the Lord first for your husband's change of heart. Your trust must remain in the Lord, not in your circumstances.
- Take the extra time and effort to *prepare physically* for your husband. Give him your very best.
- *Respect and submit* to your husband's authority and leadership. God rewards obedience.
- *Serve and honor* your husband. Allow him to be king of your home.

Does this advice sound old-fashioned? You may think these basic concepts do not apply to today's marriages. You may believe things are different today. This is a new generation, right? Are things really different? Do you truly believe men have changed? Humility will be required in order to minister to your husband effectively. There are no short-cuts.

Consider this. Will you live in disobedience like Queen Vashti and lose everything? Can't you see she turned over her home, her husband and all that was rightfully hers to another woman? Or, will you be like Queen Esther who walked in obedience and submission to her king? Both of these women were the wives of King Ahaseurus, one handling things her way and the other God's way. Is there any guess as to which one gained favor with the king and obtained the blessings of the kingdom?

Spend time in prayer. The Lord will help you develop the spirit of Queen Esther. Her strong faith and trust in God enabled her to be obedient and submissive to her husband even during very difficult circumstances. Just as she found favor with King Ahaseurus, so you too will find favor with your king.

Queen Esther had something very special which is a missing ingredient in many of today's marriages--a regard and respect for her husband's authority. This respect was reciprocated. Notice that King Ahaseurus gained a mutual respect for his queen and gave her favor.

There is an important lesson to be learned in this story. Before honor, there is always humility.

> *"Before destruction the heart of man is haughty, and before honour is humility," (Prov. 18:12).*

Queen Vashti attempted to usurp her husband's authority, and she was humbled to nothing. She lost her husband's favor and was removed from her royal place in the kingdom.

Queen Esther showed humility by her willingness to put others before herself. Her submissive and obedient spirit gained her husband's favor and advanced her to a royal place in the kingdom.

> *"Therefore I will judge you, O house of Israel, every one according to his ways, saith the Lord God. Repent, and turn yourselves from all your transgressions; so*

iniquity shall not be your ruin. Cast away from you all your transgressions, whereby ye have transgressed; and make you a new heart and a new spirit: for why will ye die, O house of Israel?" (Ezek. 18:30-31).

I ask you, wounded wife, *"For why will ye die?"* Why do you continue to let your marriage die? Repent. The Lord will *"make you a new heart and a new spirit."* Do not look at submission to your husband as the stepping stone to your destruction. It is not.

"Because he considereth, and turneth away from all his transgressions that he hath committed, he shall surely live, he shall not die," (Ezek. 18:28).

"For I have no pleasure in the death of him that dieth, saith the Lord God: wherefore turn yourselves, and live ye," (Ezek. 18:32).

Choose life. Submitting to your husband is the propelling force to your victory, resulting in a happy and healthy marriage, a marriage where you can serve as queen.

You may continue to argue that I do not know your husband or the conditions you are living in. You are absolutely right. I don't. All of us have our own battle scars of varying degrees. The truth is there is only one person who knows every private detail. He is all you need. Trust Jesus. He is able to transform your husband into a man worthy of honor and respect, a king you can truly admire and trust.

CHAPTER ELEVEN
HARDEN NOT YOUR HEARTS!

As a Pastor's secretary for many years, I observed married couples of varying ages as they came into our church office for marital counseling. Some tried to cover and hide their emotional distress with a façade. A variety of adjectives could be used to describe most of the others. They were upset, distraught, nervous, angry, frustrated, critical, depressed, unforgiving, flippant, haughty, shocked, downcast, bitter, hardhearted and desperate. Though the common denominator for all was a troubled marriage, their responses varied.

I noticed, in many instances, struggling couples were only hoping to find confirmation their marriages were over. It was as if they needed the counselor's blessing on their decision to end their marital relationships. The last thing they wanted or expected to hear from a counselor was to go home and begin working on their marriages, marriages they had already pronounced dead in their hearts. They often left the counselor's office angry, with assignments they were unwilling to complete or with advice they were unwilling to apply. It was no wonder counseling did them little good. Observers could easily recognize those having hard hearts, even though they did their very best to cleverly conceal them.

Of course, there were always those precious few who sincerely desired to reconcile their differences. Their hungry hearts pleased the Lord as they sought Him for answers regarding their marital relationships, and they were obedient to instruction. They were willing to make any changes necessary to save their marriages.

Do you find yourself becoming increasingly disheartened with your marriage or unanswered prayers? Are you giving up on God? Are you taking matters into your own hands? Has your heart become hardened? Do you realize the consequences of a hard heart?

Paul speaks of *"hardening not your hearts"* in the Book of Hebrews. He is reminding us not to become hardhearted as did the Israelites in the day of provocation. They had turned away from God.

Do you realize how quickly we turn away from God when things get tough in our lives? As soon as we get a little uncomfortable, as soon as we do not immediately receive an answer to prayer, as soon as our marriage begins experiencing conflict, many of us become exactly like the Israelites. We take matters into our own hands.

It is so easy to look back at history and question or condemn the Israelites' behavior for turning away from God after seeing and experiencing so many miracles. Their actions show how weak humanity really is given the right circumstances and pressures. This is the exact reason why we should never judge someone for their failures. Who really knows what we would be capable of doing, given the same pressures? How would we respond, walking in their shoes?

Let us guard our hearts, so we do not become judgmental or critical. Let us guard our hearts, so we do not fall into sin or become hardhearted toward God. Let us keep our hearts pure, so we are ready to reach down and help others back up who have fallen. Let's give them the encouragement they need to continue trusting God for their situations. Are we showing mercy to others? What about compassion? Are we helping to build their faith and belief that God can do the impossible in their lives?

Any wife struggling to survive in a troubled marriage can become hardhearted if she does not carefully guard her heart. You may have been standing on one of God's promises for years. Time keeps passing by. You have truly wanted to believe God, but your circumstances never change or improve. You begin questioning and doubting God. Discouragement begins to move in. Before long, you find yourself putting the promise aside and, in a short time, altogether forgetting the promise God made to you. After deception finally takes its filthy grip, you begin rebelling and taking matters into your own hands, just as the Israelites did during the provocation. It is critically important you guard your heart so this chain of events can be avoided in your life.

> "Wherefore (as the Holy Ghost saith, Today if ye will hear his voice, Harden not your hearts, as in the provocation, in the day of temptation in the wilderness: When your fathers tempted me, proved me, and saw my works forty years. Wherefore I was grieved with that generation, and said, They do always err in their

heart; and they have not known my ways. So I sware to my wrath, They shall not enter into my rest.) Take heed, brethren, lest there be in any of you an evil heart of unbelief, in departing from the living God. But exhort one another daily, while it is called Today; lest any of you be hardened through the deceitfulness of sin. For we are made partakers of Christ, if we hold the beginning of our confidence stedfast unto the end; While it is said, Today if ye will hear his voice, harden not your hearts, as in the provocation. For some, when they had heard, did provoke; howbeit not all that came out of Egypt by Moses. But with whom was he grieved forty years? Was it not with them that had sinned, whose carcasses fell in the wilderness? And to whom sware he that they should not enter into his rest, but to them that believed not? So we see that they could not enter in because of unbelief. Let us therefore fear, lest a promise being left us of entering into his rest, any of you should seem to come short of it. For unto us was the gospel preached, as well as unto them; but the word preached did not profit them, not being mixed with faith in them that heard it," (Heb. 3:7-4:2).

You can learn from the last instructions Moses gave to the children of Israel. Moses poured his heart into the children of Israel who were twenty years old and younger. He didn't want them to end up like their fathers who all died in the wilderness. He wanted them to go in and possess their promise. He didn't want them to fall short of receiving everything God had available for them. He wanted them to have God's best. Do you fear your promise will never be fulfilled? Are you falling into unbelief? Are you giving up on God? The last instructions Moses gave to the children of Israel still apply to all of us today.

Moses admonished the children of Israel to *remember*. He wanted them to remember they were alive because they had cleaved to the Lord. He wanted them to remember what their eyes had seen and to keep and obey the statutes and judgments they had been taught.

Moses also instructed them to *take heed*, which means to beware. He knew how quickly they could forget all they had seen. They could easily forget all God had done for them, where He had brought them from, and everything He had taught them. Moses had invested his life into instructing them, and they knew the laws of God. He realized, however, the laws could quickly depart from their hearts, leaving them in the same condition as their rebellious fathers.

Their fathers had provoked God. They were called a lying people. Ezekiel called them impudent and hardhearted. They were immovable, having no regard for other people's feelings. They were idolaters, perverse and crooked. They were deaf and blind, refusing to hear and not observing what they saw. They were foolish and unwise, living a life of vanity. They were adamant, having hearts so hard they could not be penetrated. They were self-willed, stiff-necked, faithless, stubborn, stiff-hearted, haughty, adulterers, rebellious, wicked and corrupt.

In the Book of Hebrews, it is interesting to note that Paul was speaking to believers, not sinners. He knew believers could end up in the same sinful condition if they failed to guard their hearts. A hardened heart will not heed instruction. It will give up on the Lord performing His Word and fulfilling His promises. It will become heavy-laden and filled with unbelief and fear. It will forget all the Lord has done. Eventually, it will become filled with the deceitfulness of sin. A hardened heart will not enter into His rest.

In the days of old, the hardhearted Israelites refused to believe the land was all God had promised. Because of their lack of trust and faith in God, they sent out spies to see if the land was everything God said it would be and then still chose to believe the bad reports. They allowed fear to immobilize them, and they were not allowed into the Promised Land. In the same way, believers will miss their mark and fail to reach their land of promise, if they continue to allow themselves to be controlled by hardened hearts.

Have you known people with hearts of stone? This group is representative of those who become impatient and tired of waiting on God to answer their prayers. They lose all trust and faith in God and choose to do things their way. Without hope, they give up. These individuals are frustrated and miserable. Unless they turn around, they will lose out on spending eternity with God. Eternal life will not be their haven of rest.

Moses warned the children of Israel not to let a hard heart keep them from entering into God's rest, which was the Promised Land. In Hebrews, Paul warned believers not to let a hard heart keep them out of their future haven of rest [or eternal life].

There is also a present place of rest available for you as a believer each and every day, right where you are, regardless of what you are going through. You can experience a God-given peace and calm as if in the eye of a storm. Once again, you must guard your heart to enter into this rest. The heart is the wellspring of life (Prov. 4:23). Therefore, it is absolutely essential that you keep your heart open and pliable before God.

You may ask, "How can I guard my heart?" First, *remember* all God has already done for you and your family. Praise Him for the benefits and blessings He made possible for you, your husband and your children by dying on the Cross. Praise Him for answered prayers, salvation, healings or miracles you have received or witnessed. Reflect on the promises He has already kept for you. Remember, it is God who brought you this far. It is also God who will see you through. Secondly, *keep your heart diligent*, so that you do not forget all the Lord has done for you. Strive to keep and obey the Word of God you have been taught.

Yes, it is difficult to walk by faith into the unknown, but we serve a faithful God who fulfills all of His promises. Do not let doubt, fear and discouragement control you. Keep a right attitude toward God. He will then be able to speak to you, teach you and lead you. You will no longer flounder around in the wilderness.

Maybe you have lost faith that God's promises to you will ever come to pass. The Lord knows how you have trusted Him with your husband. He has heard your every prayer. He has seen you do everything within your power to win your husband to Christ. He knows you want your marriage healed and whole. Nevertheless, your life continues to go in circles as you wander around in the wilderness, month after month or year after year with no positive change. Don't be like the Israelites in response to your delay.

In their wandering and waiting, the Israelites were guilty of impatience, resulting in disobedience and rebellion. They began complaining that God had brought them out of Egypt to let them die in the wilderness. They felt God was going to let them fall by the sword. They had lost all hope in God. They had lost all sight of God's power. They were ready to appoint a captain and return to Egypt, if not for Moses and Aaron crying out to God on their behalf. Joshua and Caleb, two of the spies, faced the angry mob to give them a good report. They did their best to encourage them and build their faith by telling them not to worry as they declared the *"giants would be bread for them"* (Num. 14:9). Joshua and Caleb had faith to believe God, faith to see beyond their obstacles. Their message, challenging the

Israelites to believe and obey God, caused the angry, hardhearted mob to stone them.

You do not have to wonder or guess whether or not you have become hardhearted. If you are hardhearted, whenever you are challenged to obey God, it is likely you will immediately become defensive or angry. You may pretend everything is fine, but you cannot conceal a hard heart. A little observation quickly exposes it. Do you find your flesh rising up when you are called to obedience? Do you become mad or defensive when you don't get your way? Do you fear your obstacles and giants are too big to be conquered by God? Do you feel God has forgotten you or let you down? Have you lost faith? Are you tempted to run back to Egypt? Examine and prove your own self. Do you still believe?

> *"Examine yourselves, whether ye be in the faith; prove your own selves...,"* (2 Cor. 13:5).

Negativity, complaining and murmuring go right along with a hardened heart. This spirit of murmuring had entered the Israelites' camp. The people grumbled and complained that the Lord had brought them out and placed them in the hands of the Amorites so they could be destroyed. They murmured against their leaders. The spirit of murmuring was contagious, and it affected Moses' sister, Miriam. She was upset over her Ethiopian sister-in-law.

> *"Hath the Lord indeed spoken only by Moses? Hath He not spoken also by us? And the Lord heard it,"* (Num. 12:2).

Miriam was basically telling her husband that Moses wasn't the only one who heard from God, and God could speak through them just as easily. Miriam's heart had become filled with jealous venom and pride.

"…jealousy is cruel as the grave; the coals thereof are coals of fire, which hath a most vehement flame," (Song of Sol. 8:6).

As a wife, you must make sure pride does not arise and display its ugly head. *"Pride goeth before destruction and a haughty spirit before a fall"* (Prov. 16:18). The spirit of pride will always rise to the occasion if given the opportunity. Do you ever hear yourself sounding a little like Miriam? Do you ever respond negatively to your husband with something like: "If the Lord wants to tell me something, I don't have to hear it from you?" You attempt, like Miriam, to usurp his spiritual authority. Where do you think that spirit of pride comes from? Do you believe you are more spiritual? Do you believe God speaks to you more clearly?

At times, do you wonder why the Lord continues to bless your husband? Does jealousy or envy rise because God uses him in spite of his past failures? You may find yourself wanting to take control and wishing the Lord would use you to lead and direct your family. This sin of pride did not go unnoticed by God in Miriam's life, and it will not go unnoticed in your life. God hears all and sees all, and there are no secrets from God. Everything is laid bare and opened before the eyes of God (Heb. 4:13).

This attitude of heart will never help your situation or heal your marriage. The Lord heard Miriam and Aaron when they questioned and criticized the one God placed in authority. Good consequences will never be the end result of questioning God's authority. For Miriam, her behavior resulted in separation from God and leprosy. Thankfully, Moses cried out to God for her healing. Take note that there were consequences to Miriam's sinful behavior.

I have overheard many "Miriams" through the years. I have heard women tear down their husbands, complaining and murmuring to their faces as well as behind their backs.

They, like Miriam, wanted to lead. They continually challenged the authority God had placed in their homes. This murmuring carried over into other areas of their lives as well, i.e. their families, their churches, their jobs.

I have heard wives curse their husbands from A to Z in many public places. Their agitation seemed to grow when not being given the reins to lead. They did not see the error of their own ways. Sometimes, they quietly displayed their dissatisfaction with a sigh, a deep breath or a cutting eye. Let's remember God hates pride, and considers jealousy as the sin of witchcraft.

A hardened heart will eventually reap a harvest, one of eternal hardness. It will stop paying attention and is no longer interested in what God is saying. It will produce misery and strife wherever it goes, thus driving people away from Christ. In contrast, a soft heart wants to hear and understand what God is saying and it is willing to obey. A pure heart and right attitude will draw people to Christ.

Do you fear your heart has become hardened? Do you fear you have been driving your husband away from God rather than to Him? It is not too late to make things right. All you have to do is repent, and you will put a stop to this wilderness experience in your life.

As you put your trust in Jesus, you will begin to see your giants as small in the hands of a mighty and awesome God. It is time for you to go in and possess your promise.

"Today, if you will hear His voice, harden not your hearts!"

CHAPTER TWELVE
TO A WOMAN WHO HAS AN EAR - LET HER HEAR!

Good communication is important in marriage. Your husband may be talking, but are you listening? Are you hearing what he is saying to you? A man is going to want to vent his thoughts somewhere. Be a ready listener and slow to speak (James 1:19). Learn to be a good sounding board. Set an atmosphere in your home where your husband can talk to you. Show an interest in his day.

While spending "quality" time with our husbands, are we guilty of multitasking? Are we reading a book, texting, messaging Facebook friends or watching TV at the same time? Put down your smart phones. My husband wants my undivided attention. What about yours? I think it's funny because he can be watching TV and may not be giving me his full attention, but he will surely notice the minute I am not giving him my full attention. If you want to productively converse with your husband, he must know you are only interested in him at that moment.

Your husband needs to feel free to share his thoughts without the anticipation of criticism or rejection. Don't try to correct your husband or take over the conversation. Don't even suggest ways that might be of help to him unless he specifically asks for help. This might be difficult for you, but your husband is an adult, not a child. Allow him the freedom to have his own opinions and learning experiences. Too often, wives try to protect their husbands from failure, as they would a child, thus stunting their character development.

My Dad did not take time to read instructions. He would begin putting a project together on his own. My sweet mother would read the instruction booklet and stand nearby anticipating his need of help. I was often amazed at her silence. She didn't volunteer her assistance even when she had a solution to his dilemma. My Dad would struggle to put things together for hours, always ending up with extra parts. In the end, he would grab the booklet and read it himself. Once in a great while, he would ask for her help. If he did, she was ready. I asked her one day why she didn't offer to help. Her answer was simple, "Daddy don't need my help. He will have that fixed in a minute." She was a wise woman. She knew in order for him to experience a sense of accomplishment that he needed to complete the job himself. She would then inflate his ego with praise for a job well done.

The truth is that my mother was probably more capable in the fix-it department. Her father had taught her how to repair many small appliances around the house. My Dad didn't have the same privilege. Mom's patience helped him to grow and become more proficient at many skills.

Consider this. If your boss were speaking to you, would you interrupt with your ideas or criticize or reject his plans? No! Instead, you would give his ideas strong consideration, looking for ways to help them come to pass. You would try to make his vision your vision. You would probably show your interest and approval. In the same way, your husband needs to know you are on his team. He needs to know you share his excitement and enthusiasm.

Don't allow your husband's conversation to stir up worry or nervousness in you. In my experience, men seem to handle problems when they arise, but women are more likely to devote their energies into the prevention of problems. Many times, we look past the present and see potential disaster. Don't fall apart. [I am preaching this to myself.] If you allow your emotions to run wild and you get all upset and panic, your husband will quit sharing with you. If your husband is open enough to share a problem he is having, he probably needs your love, understanding, strength and encouragement. Don't allow fear to destroy that intimate moment.

Be a good and interested listener. Keep your silence. Many women ramble, and their poor husbands are not given opportunities to share their thoughts. A man will never compete with a rambling wife. His thoughts lose their importance when he feels he has to compete.

My husband and I were having dinner one night with guests, and a very mild-mannered man attempted several times to speak to my husband. Every time he opened his mouth, his wife would interrupt him, interject her thoughts and take control of the conversation. She would ramble on and on. She would complete his sentences, not allowing him the privilege of completing one thought. All night long, no one could get one word in edgewise. This woman did all the talking, and everyone at the table became frustrated and uncomfortable. This husband had resolved to give up, sit back and stay quiet rather than fight his wife for an opportunity to speak.

A woman guided by prudence knows not to talk too much, and *"a prudent wife is from the Lord"* (Prov. 19:14). She allows wisdom to guide her as to when to keep silent and when to speak.

Be satisfied with the information you are given. It is natural for women to desire details. Men, for the most part, are not interested in hearing or knowing all the details. If you keep pumping your husband for details, he will eventually become aggravated and clam up. This is probably my hardest battle in communication because I am a "detail" person. My husband may just want to give me the "what," and I want him to share the entire story from beginning to end. I pressed him one night, and his reply was, "I guess next time I will have to take notes." Oops!

Recognize that it is okay to have two different viewpoints. You will not always approach things in the same way. My eight year-old granddaughter put it perfectly when my son didn't understand why she approached something a certain way. She answered, "Daddy, you have your brain and I have mine." How true! John and I tease sometimes by repeating her comment to each other.

Your husband needs to know he can count on you to keep his most intimate thoughts confidential. Not only will sharing his confidences upset him, but he will begin to keep things to himself. You want to avoid him seeking another sounding board he can trust. Should you urgently need to confide in someone for prayer or counsel, be sure to choose that person very carefully. Choose someone whose advice you can trust. Choose someone who has your best interest at heart. Choose someone who will tell you the truth even when it hurts.

Your husband needs to know you take every word he speaks seriously. He wants to be No. 1 in your eyes, and this is confirmed when you receive everything he says to you as important. This honor and admiration will make him feel like a king. Pay special attention to your husband's requests. He will know you are listening to him by your obedience to the "little" things. My husband's face lights up when he realizes I responded to a comment he made very casually, especially when he thought he did not have my full attention.

Learn to build your husband's ego. A man's ego is probably one of his greatest weaknesses. He will look for someone to build his ego and make him feel important. Make sure that someone is you.

All of us have been negative from time to time, so let's work on being more positive. No one wants to listen to a negative person. Being negative will repel even those who love you. On the other hand, being positive will attract and draw those you love. There was a time that negativity on his job actually cost a co-worker the loss of respect from his peers. They dodged him and no longer included him. They were tired of hearing why every idea would not work. Have you ever been around a negative person? I have. It is no fun. A negative person continues to see the glass half empty and refuses to see it half full. Working to convert negative viewpoints to positive can make you feel like you are in the middle of a battle. This type of conversation can be exhausting. *The Little Engine That Could* had the better attitude.

Listening may sometimes require "listening beyond or between the lines" of words being spoken. Ask yourself why your husband often brings up the same issue. What is he really trying to say? If you are hearing the same little innuendos over and over, you can be assured this is something you should give special attention.

One evening, as my husband and I sat down to enjoy a movie together, the buzzer went off on our dryer. I removed the clothes from the dryer and began to fold them while I was sitting there next to him. It seemed like a good use of my time. I never dreamed it would matter to him. I heard, "Folding clothes again, huh?" A few days later, something similar happened, and I heard him mumble, "Always have clothes to fold?" I turned to him and asked if it bothered him. He asked, "Can't you do that some other time?"

Don't you love when your husband answers your question with a question? Obviously, he was looking forward to a little "TLC," and I was busying myself with everything but him. I learned the importance of giving him quality time. After all, didn't I want quality time from him?

You are married to a unique individual. Yes, it is truly possible to converse with the man you love. He will have certain topics he really enjoys talking about as well as areas he would rather leave alone. In my case, I am amazed at how much my husband has to say when he is around another hunter. They share common ground with a sport they love. I may never be a deer slayer, but I can still share in my husband's excitement and discussion of a topic he loves.

Always remember the eyes are a window to the soul. Learn to look directly into his eyes when he is speaking to you. This shows he has your undivided attention and you are interested in what he is saying. This will help to produce intimacy in your marriage.

Unfortunately, there are times we are guilty of putting too much pressure on our husbands. Have you ever pushed your husband to complete a project in the heat of the summer or after he had already put in a 60-hour work week?

When you make a request of him and you hear words like "just give it to the mule" or "add it to my list," this should clearly signal he needs some rest--and it is probably long overdue. Guard the requests you make of him.

He wants to please you, and he wants to believe he can still do everything he did when he was eighteen and in the best shape of his life. He will push and push, sometimes edging beyond his limits. Don't be selfish. Be sensitive enough to realize when your requests are sapping his strength, robbing him of the rest he needs, or in the long run, negatively affecting his health. When he prefers to postpone a project, don't automatically assume procrastination or laziness. It may be his way of saying he is physically or mentally tired and worn out. Allow him the privilege of listening to his own body. Your love should be demonstrated by putting his well-being and care before your own selfish desires.

Every man wants a wife to appreciate him. I can't stress enough the importance of appreciating your husband. Show him you love him by having a heart of gratitude and thankfulness. Let him know how much you need him and how very important he is to you. Thank him for the little things he does for you on a daily basis. Appreciate the gifts he gives you even if they are not exactly what you would have purchased. Admire him for the way he handles situations that arise with others. As you practice listening, you might be pleasantly surprised how much more you will come to love, appreciate and respect your husband.

"To a woman who has an ear, let her hear!"

CHAPTER THIRTEEN
THE TONGUE IS A FIRE!

Have you ever struggled to hold your tongue? You may have known the precise thing to say, but before you could manage your tongue, you blurted out something inappropriate. Your words could have been unkind, worthless remarks. Even more unfortunate, they could have been the evil thoughts you had been storing and hiding in your heart.

Regretfully, you might have even asked yourself later, "Why did I make such a dreadful comment?" Or, "Where did those ugly words come from?" Like the Apostle Paul, when you desire to do well, is evil right there with you (Rom. 7:18-21)? Is controlling your tongue one of your greatest struggles?

Responding to circumstances, no doubt, poorly reflected my walk of faith. The Lord had been teaching me the value of praising, encouraging and supporting my husband. I had been working diligently to be in command of my tongue, to speak words of faith, affirmation and edification. I wanted to be led by the Holy Spirit. I did not want circumstances to dictate my actions and responses. I had already wasted far too much time in a negative direction and was finally beginning to understand the great value of speaking life into my marriage. Death and life are in the power of the tongue. We will indulge in the consequences of our words, whether death or life (Prov. 18:20-21). By our words, we will be justified and acquitted, and by our words, we will be condemned and sentenced (Matt. 12:37).

As you might guess, right about the time I felt I was making considerable progress, here came a test. One evening, my husband didn't come home from work on time nor did he call to say he would be late. He was usually hungry when he arrived home and would know dinner was on the stove and ready. His routine was fairly predictable, and this was not the norm. At first, like most wives, I gave him the benefit of the doubt. I thought he was probably detained in traffic, and I waited patiently. As time passed, my patience turned to worry. I wondered if he was in an accident, and I waited nervously. After quite a few hours passed and dinner was cold and ruined, I waited angrily.

Somehow, my worry about a traffic accident turned into an upsetting hunch he was most likely with his co-workers having a few drinks after work. My French temper intensified with every ticking minute. Why couldn't he get the victory in this area of his life? He had been doing so much better. He had started going to church, he seemed to enjoy the services, and he had started reading his Bible. Now this! What a disappointment. My greatest desire was to see him on fire for God. Trying to serve God while seeing how close to the world he could live would never work. Didn't he realize he could not serve two masters? Didn't he want to live under the blessings and favor of God? How could he serve the Lord if the world still had a grasp on him? Why wouldn't he walk away from his old life?

Pacing and praying consumed my time and energy. I knew I had to mitigate what my anger was calling me to do. Reacting was not the answer, so I prayed for self-control. Controlling my temper and welcoming him home with love, although admittedly difficult, would allow the Lord to work in his heart. However, if he was verbally attacked, he would respond to the attack, justify his sinful actions, and completely shut his heart to the wooing of the Holy Spirit. I had to learn to stay out of God's way. In times past, I had been guilty of interfering, thinking the Lord was moving too slowly or not at all. I always ended up doing things my way. This was a mistake that I didn't want to make again.

If the Word of God was actively working in my life, my controlled response had to be to the Word of God rather than to the negative situation. To do this, anger had to die. My flesh had to be crucified. Remaining quiet and giving him time to explain would achieve better results than an attack. This response could even lead to repentance. I knew I should be swift to hear, slow to speak and slow to wrath. I knew my wrath would not produce righteousness (James 1:19-20). I finally calmed down and truly thought I was geared up and ready to respond correctly regardless of his demeanor when he entered the house.

The sound of the car engine alerted me to his arrival, and the front door began to open slowly. He came in, walked directly toward me, and kissed me hello, as if he had done nothing wrong. Pugh! I could smell the alcohol on his breath. My "gut" feeling had become a reality. My heart was sick, and I was saddened because he didn't see anything wrong with what he had done. Why was he still holding onto the world? Why wouldn't he let it go? How could he do such a thing to the Lord? Why couldn't he see that he was hurting me? I wanted so much better for him. There was no explanation good enough. I was angry. The bomb that had been ticking inside me for the past several hours exploded.

Thank the Lord I had prayed. Can you imagine how awful it might have been had I not prayed? That is why God's Word says:

> *"It is better to dwell in the wilderness, than with a contentious and an angry woman," (Prov. 21:19).*

My flesh had taken total control--again. I didn't stop running my mouth until my basket was completely emptied. Sorry to say, my tongue held nothing back. It was a tongue of fire, full of deadly poison. I had never been a cursing woman, but I still had the ability to cut him to the heart with the sharp words of my mouth. He retaliated, and things were said by both of us that took a long time to heal, words that accomplished nothing.

> *"Behold, we put bits in the horses' mouths, that they may obey us; and we turn about their whole body. Behold also the ships, which though they be so great, and are driven of fierce winds, yet are they turned about with a very small helm, whithersoever the governor listeth. Even so the tongue is a little member, and boasteth great things. Behold, how great a matter a little fire kindleth! And the tongue is a fire, a world of iniquity; so is the tongue among our members, that it defileth the whole body, and setteth on fire the course of nature; and it is set on fire of hell," (James 3:3-6).*

Afterwards, I felt ashamed for the hurtful things I had said. I had definitely not handled this situation correctly. I am certain my actions did not please God. Once again, I had taken the reins back to handle the situation myself rather than trusting my husband to the Lord. I knew better. I knew it was better for me to hold my tongue, love him, pray for him and trust the Lord to convict him of sin. When would I ever learn to stay out of God's business? When would I ever learn to let God be God? I knew holding my tongue was wise (Prov. 10:19), I knew guarding my mouth would keep me from calamity (Prov. 21:23), and I knew if I loved life and desired to see many good days, I needed to keep my tongue from evil (Psa. 34:12-13). Nevertheless, on this particular day, I failed miserably.

Have you ever heard the old adage, "A man convinced against his will is of the same opinion still?" I realized any change my husband made in his life for the sole purpose of pleasing me would not last. This type of change would only be short-lived. Any change he made to relieve my nagging and anger or to stop my tears would only be temporary. He needed a true heart change. However, if I would allow the Lord to do the changing, the change would bring about repentance. The change would be lasting. That is what I really wanted--a permanent change. It wouldn't matter if I was with him or away from him. His own godly convictions would be his guide and dictate his behavior. Only the Lord could bring about this type of permanent heart change. I had to keep trusting and believing God. What a relief to not have the responsibility of being the gatekeeper.

The following is a story as it was told to me, and it is certain to build your faith as it did mine.

Once upon a time, there was a sweet Christian lady whose husband drank on a daily basis. He drank until he was obnoxious, and then he would find his way back home. She very lovingly received him home, prepared his meal and served him with honor. She didn't raise her voice, attack him in anger or preach to him that he was going to hell. Instead, with a meek and quiet spirit, she showed him kindness, gentleness and love. She opened her mouth with wisdom, and in her tongue was the law of kindness (Prov. 31:26).

One afternoon at the bar, the men were laughing, joking and making fun of their annoyed and angry wives. This man began telling his friends how wonderful his wife was to him. One of his drinking buddies asked if he could go home with him to see for himself. This sounded too good to be true. The man brought his friend home and entered his house. Desiring to show off in front of his friend, he demanded his wife hurry to the kitchen to fix both of them something to eat. The wife kissed and hugged her husband, told him how happy she was he was home safely, welcomed his friend, and began preparing a banquet dinner fit for a king.

This precious woman sang in the kitchen as she cooked. She was pleasant and full of joy. With a great big smile, she served them a delicious meal. She had learned a valuable lesson in life. Her difficult circumstances did not dictate her joy. It came from heaven above. Her husband's drunken stupor and sinful condition could not steal her joy. Her husband had not put the joy in her heart, and her husband could not take it away. Her joy came from the Lord.

The husband left the table for a moment, and the friend asked, "Ma'am, may I ask you a few questions? All the men at the bar go home to angry wives, and your husband said you were different. I asked to come home with him just to prove him wrong. You are different. Why didn't you get angry when he surprised you by bringing me here? Why didn't you fuss when he demanded you fix us something to eat? How can you be so good to us when we don't deserve your goodness?"

She replied, "You see, sir, I love my husband. His friends are always welcome in our home. My husband does not know my Jesus, and he will not come to church with me or read the Word of God. I pray for him daily. I have realized I might be the only Jesus he may ever meet, so I pray each day I will be so full of Jesus that His love can flow out of me and touch my husband's heart. I hope, sir, the Jesus in me has touched your heart today as well because Jesus loves you too." Her answer was full of grace and seasoned with salt (Col. 4:6).

There is a powerful lesson in this heartwarming testimony. Jesus is gracious and compassionate. He is slow to anger and rich in love. He is good to all, and He has compassion on all He has made (Psa. 145:8-9). This wife was full of Jesus, and it was Jesus who flowed out of her. Is the love of Jesus shining through you? If you are the only Jesus your husband sees, I am sure you will want him to see a Jesus who loves him, forgives him and cares for him.

The words and manner in which you speak and the way you respond to your husband will make quite a difference in the mood you set in your home. You have more power than you realize. You have the power and ability to create a calm, pleasant and cheery atmosphere or you can make your home a place of anguish, despair and misery. Your words can pierce like a sword or bring healing (Prov. 12:18). Choose to speak words of healing.

An uncontrolled tongue pouring out fiery darts, evil and cutting words of retaliation and words of death will never bring healing to a troubled home. In anger, you will say reckless and harmful words you don't mean. Blurting out everything you want to say--words you will not be able to take back--will cause deep wounds. Why add fuel to your fire?

> *"For a good tree bringeth not forth corrupt fruit; neither doth a corrupt tree bring forth good fruit. For every tree is known by his own fruit. For of thorns men do not gather figs, nor of a bramble bush gather they grapes. A good man out of the good treasure of his*

heart bringeth forth that which is good; and an evil man out of the evil treasure of his heart bringeth forth that which is evil: for of the abundance of the heart his mouth speaketh," (Luke 6:43-45).

Speak words that will soothe, calm and heal, words of love and blessing. Speak words that will be positive, uplifting and life-giving. Guarding your tongue will aid you in bringing peace and contentment into your home. Health and refreshing will come from words spoken at the right moment. Your wise answers will bring joy (Prov. 15:23).

As you put God's Words into your heart, begin to speak His Word and promises by faith. His Word will renew your mind and change the way you think. Make no mistake! Your thoughts can either positively or negatively affect who you are and how you will respond to others.

"For as he thinks in his heart, so is he," (Prov. 23:7).

You should never underestimate the creative power of your words. You have the power, through your words, to breathe life and healing into your marriage.

Choose life!

CHAPTER FOURTEEN
A WOMAN'S INFLUENCE

Seeing your husband on fire for God is certain to be a desire close to your heart. You want to see him accept his leadership role in every aspect of his life--home, church and work. You pray the Lord mold him into the image of Christ. This is every Christian wife's prayer.

As you review the following qualities of a spiritual leader (Tit. 1:6-9; 1 Tim. 3:2-13), take time to examine your own heart. Are you helping promote spiritual growth in your husband? Or, might you be hindering his spiritual growth as priest of his home?

Please ask yourself, "What can I do to be a better wife?" Don't kid yourself. You are a woman with tremendous influence and power. His heart is like a pendulum. It can either swing toward God or away from Him. Are your actions drawing him closer to God or pushing him farther away? If you have been working hard in an attempt to change your husband, stop. Instead, strive to be a better wife. Concentrate on making changes in your own life, in any areas needing improvement. Let's look closely at these qualities of a spiritual leader.

A godly leader should be *blameless,* living his life without reproach or disgrace, without scandal.

- Do you hold your husband in a place of honor or do you belittle him?
- Do you compliment and praise him or do you criticize him in public?
- Do you bring him disgrace, tarnishing his character by ungodly conduct or dress, sinful habits or by the words you speak?
- Do you have a meek and quiet spirit or are you loud, bold or *hot*-tempered?
- Have you forgiven him or do you continue to remind him of past sins?
- Do you air his "dirty laundry" to others or do you stand your ground in defending his reputation?

"A virtuous woman is a crown to her husband; but she that maketh ashamed is as rottenness in his bones," (Prov. 12:4).

A godly leader should be a *husband of one wife.*

- Do you do your best to meet all of his needs, emotionally, physically and spiritually?
- Are you pleasant to live with, by being happy, good-natured and rested?

- Do you fill your home with laughter?
- Do you submit to his authority?
- Do you give him special attention?
- Are you a good listener?
- Do you show him he is the No. 1 love in your life?
- Do you obey his requests?

A godly leader should be *vigilant*, alertly watchful to avoid the snares of Satan.

- Do you discuss your feelings or "female intuition" openly, without fear and panic?
- Do you help him to guard himself and to be attentive and alert?
- Do you pray for your husband daily?

A godly leader should be *sober and temperate*.

- Do you allow him time to think things through or do you push him into making quick, rash decisions?
- Do you do your best to keep things pleasant and calm at home?

A godly leader should be a man of *good behavior*.

- Do you encourage and motivate him to do good, provoking him to good works?
- Do you give him honor?
- Do you admire and praise him for his godly character?
- Do you criticize him for being too conservative?

A godly leader is *given to hospitality*, readily receptive and generous.

- Do you allow your husband the privilege of inviting guests home?
- Is the house well-kept so as not to embarrass your husband?
- Do you have something available to offer your guests, i.e. coffee, snacks?
- Do you appreciate his kindness toward others and his willingness to share and socialize?
- Are you an attentive hostess to his guests?

A godly leader is *apt to teach* or able and willing to communicate the knowledge God has given him.

- Do you set an atmosphere in the home conducive to prayer and Bible study?
- Do you honor him and recognize his authority by being an attentive listener?
- When he is sharing with others, do you offer your support and respect?
- Do you rudely interrupt him to correct or "say your piece?"

A godly leader is *not given to wine*.

- Are you living by strong, godly convictions?
- Do you prayerfully keep all doors closed so the enemy will not have entrance into your home and family?

"Wine is a mocker, strong drink is raging: and whosoever is deceived thereby is not wise," (Prov. 20:1).

A godly leader is *no striker*, not quarrelsome with hands.

- Do you keep your husband agitated and frustrated by your railing or hostile attitude?
- Do you help keep peace in your home?
- Do you keep your hands to yourself and refrain from getting physical when angry?
- Do you maintain self-control?

A godly leader is *not greedy of filthy lucre* or not covetous of money or profit.

- Do you continually bring up items you would like to purchase but cannot afford?
- Do you complain about your husband's provisions for the family?
- Do you run up bills he cannot pay, causing him to become a scrooge rather than a cheerful giver?

"The heart of her husband doth safely trust in her, so that he shall have no need of spoil," (Prov. 31:11).

A godly leader is *patient*.

- Do you allow him to be tolerant and longsuffering with people?
- Do you often complain that people are taking advantage of his goodness?
- Do you praise him when you recognize patience at work in his life?

A godly leader is *not a brawler,* not quarrelsome with his tongue.

- Does he have to fuss to get your attention?
- Must he get angry before you will yield to his wishes?
- Do you provoke arguments?

- Do you allow him the privilege of having the last word?
- Do you argue until he gives up and you win? Even if you win, you lose.

A godly leader is *not covetous* and does not desire what belongs to another.

COVETING – AN INWARD DESIRE OF THE HEART--LONGING FOR, SCHEMING AND PUTTING FORTH ANY EFFORT TO ACQUIRE SOMETHING THAT BELONGS TO ANOTHER.

- Do you make him aware you are happy with his provisions?
- Do you help him to plan, budget and save so he can afford some things he desires?
- Do you add undue stress by wanting to keep up with the Jones'?

A godly leader is *one that rules his house well.*

- Do you obey and submit to your husband's authority?
- Do you allow him to lead your family?
- Do you commend him for his good, sound decisions?
- Do you recognize that his authority in the home has been given to him by God?
- Have you learned to be content when you hear the word *"no?"*

A godly leader's *children are in subjection with all gravity.* In other words, his children hold him in a place of honor and high esteem, and they respect he holds a position of importance.

- Do you build dad up to your children as *"king and priest"* of your home?
- Do you obey his wishes even when he is not present?
- Do you argue and tear down each other in front of your children?
- Do you ever criticize your husband or speak negatively about him to your children in his presence or behind his back?
- Do you honor him, giving him praise and thanks, in your children's presence?
- When your husband disciplines your children, do the children know daddy has mom's full support?

A godly leader is *not a novice*. He is one who knows in whom and what he believes. By sound doctrine, he may exhort, convince and rebuke those in opposition of truth.

- Do you ask him to help you understand the Word of God, even when you can study on your own?
- Do you work together to memorize Scripture?
- Do you stir up an eagerness and interest in the pursuit of Christ and the things of God?
- Do you allow him a quiet time to pray or read and study God's Word?

A godly leader is of a *good report*.

- Do you defend your husband's reputation?
- Do you realize you are a direct reflection and expression of your husband?
- Would your dress and conduct in public represent your husband well? Your children's?

- Do you show friendliness by doing good deeds and labors of love?
- Do you get along well with others?

A godly leader is *grave*, important and a man of dignity.

- Is he a man of importance in your life?
- Do you give serious consideration to the words he speaks?
- Do you teach your children daddy will make decisions based on what is right before God and best for the family?
- Do your children know, by your example, how important daddy is to the family?

A godly leader is *not double-tongued.*

- Are you honest and a woman of integrity?
- Do you put your husband in awkward positions by spreading lies or gossip?
- Do you praise him for his integrity?
- Do you say what you really mean?
- Do you keep your word and help him to keep his?
- Do you frustrate him with a constant undercurrent in the home where your actions are sending a different message than your words?

A godly leader is one of *pure conscience.* A pure conscience preserves our souls.

- Do you bring up failures and stir up guilt?
- Do you help him to forget the past and press forward with God?
- Has he received your forgiveness?

A godly leader possesses *boldness in the faith*. Integrity and decency will promote boldness in the faith.

- Do you encourage your husband to share his faith with others?
- When he does, are you guilty of jumping in, correcting or making him look foolish?
- Do you rejoice with him when he wins someone to the Lord?

A godly leader is a *steward of God*.

- Do you encourage and support his involvement of time, talent and money?
- Do you work as a team, offering your help and support?

A godly leader is *not self-willed*.

- Do you praise him for his self-sacrificing devotion?
- Do you discourage him from doing for others?
- Are you guilty of pushing him to take care of his own needs first, causing him to put the needs of others last on his list?

A godly leader is *not soon angry*.

- Do you remain calm and mild-mannered?
- Do you encourage a forgiving spirit?
- Do you try your best to be understanding?
- Do you control your temper?
- Do you hold your tongue?

A godly leader is a *lover of good men*.

- Do you praise his choice of wise, godly friends?

- Do you allow him time for fellowship?

"He that walketh with wise men shall be wise; but a companion of fools shall be destroyed," (Prov. 13:20).

A godly leader is *just*.

- Do you let him know you notice when he exercises fairness?
- Do you appreciate him for being impartial, honest, truthful and moral?

A godly leader is *holy*.

- Do you thank him for believing in Jesus Christ as his Lord and Savior and for leading his family to believe?
- Do you praise him and honor him for living a godly life and for keeping his heart pure before God?
- Do you respect him as the spiritual priest of your home, giving him grace, if he is a diamond in the rough?
- Do you pray with him and for him?

The purpose of studying these qualities cannot and should not be an attempt to manipulate your husband. Manipulation is a sin and is a form of witchcraft.

<u>MANIPULATION</u> - TO CONTROL BY UNFAIR OR INSIDIOUS MEANS TO ONE'S OWN ADVANTAGE.

As a result of this study, however, you will begin to recognize godly characteristics as they develop and grow into a part of your husband's character. This will build your faith and renew your hope. Learning these qualities will also make you more aware of areas where you fall short as a supportive wife.

A wife has tremendous power to influence her husband for good or evil. As a godly wife, you want to encourage and promote your husband's spiritual growth, not hinder it. There's no condemnation in Christ. As the Holy Spirit reveals areas to you that need some attention, why don't you repent and begin working on those areas? The Lord will give you creative and imaginative ideas which will enable you to better serve, encourage and honor your husband.

It is thrilling to see the Spirit of God at work. You will be amazed at the positive changes in your lives as you allow the Lord to take the lead. Day by day, your excitement will increase as you experience the Spirit of God at work in you, your husband, your marriage and your home.

> *"…Not by might, nor by power, but by my spirit, saith the Lord of hosts," (Zech. 4:6).*

CHAPTER FIFTEEN
HAVE YOU FORGIVEN?

God's Word teaches it is the responsibility of the older women to teach the younger women. Therefore, it is my duty to teach the younger women about something I know well--the power of forgiveness. The application of what you are about to read saved our marriage--and it can save yours. None of us are above failure. My inability to forgive would have locked my husband in a prison and thrown away the key. It would have been one of the key ingredients to the final destruction of our family.

Forgiveness, on the other hand, removed our marriage from the devil's grasp and placed it into the hands of the King of Kings and Lord of Lords. With a few words of forgiveness that took only a few minutes to speak, my marriage changed hands from the kingdom of Satan to the kingdom of God. With those words, we joined God's team. Forgiveness is powerful. As you gain a better understanding of the mighty power of forgiveness, it is my prayer you will forgive your spouse, releasing him and entrusting him to Almighty God.

Un-forgiveness is not only brewing in homes, but also in the workplace, in schools, as well as in churches.

There are *two aspects of forgiveness:*

1. There is the person who caused the hurt, who is in desperate need of forgiveness.
2. There is the victim who needs to forgive and release, who is in desperate need of healing.

More and more marriages are falling by the wayside because one spouse refuses to forgive the other. Individuals live hopeless lives, feeling unworthy and bound to their past failures. Either the person they hurt will not forgive them or they will not forgive themselves.

Have you ever thought the following?

- *"He doesn't deserve to be forgiven."*
- *"It may take some time, but I'll get him back."*
- *"I've given him all the chances he deserves."*
- *"He should pay for what he has done."*
- *"I'll forgive, but I'll never forget."*
- *"I'll forgive, but I'll never trust him again."*
- *"I don't have to put up with this. I'm better than that."*

Making a decision to stand involves forgiveness. Forgiveness occurs over 140 times in the New Testament. The meaning of *forgiveness* is two-fold:

1. TO GRANT RELIEF FROM A DEBT.
2. TO CEASE TO HOLD RESENTMENT AGAINST.

You may be quick to grant relief from a debt. Your spouse may apologize for hurting you, and you will respond, "Forget it. Don't worry about it." However, the second part of forgiveness is not so easy. By the time you get home, you're already talking to yourself. "He really hurt my feelings. Did you hear how he spoke to me? I didn't deserve to be treated that way." Resentment begins building in your heart.

Do you ever deceive yourself into believing you have forgiven and yet are still controlled by resentment? Even though you may be a believer, there is a good chance you do not always handle your feelings by taking them to Jesus first. Instead, you may begin stuffing all that hostility and resentment down deep into your heart, hoping nobody will ever know it is there. One day, I promise it will surface. Something will happen that will set you off. All those hurts you stuffed way down into the bottom of your basket will come back up and make a show. That show will not be pretty.

Have you--or someone you've known--ever said, "I have forgiven, but I'll never forget?" If you have been telling yourself you have forgiven and still harbor resentment in your heart, you are lying to yourself. If you have ever been around someone who repeatedly brings up an old hurt, recognize that this person's life is still being controlled by un-forgiveness. God's forgiveness ceases to hold resentment against another. Therefore, if you are having a difficult time letting go, you have not totally released that person from their sin against you.

Think about a deep puncture wound. I had surgery on both of my feet years ago. They looked like an alligator took bites out of my heels. Doctors did not want the wounds to scab over quickly. Why? It is better that deep wounds heal slowly from the inside out. If not, infection can develop underneath. No one sees it. No one realizes it is there. Yet, it grows and worsens. As soon as the scab is bumped, all the stinky, disgusting infection begins oozing out of the open sore. That is exactly how un-forgiveness works. You can put on a big smile. You can say the right things. You can hide the hurt and pain. One day, something will bump that façade loose, if your heart is not healed on the inside. The infection that you tried so hard to cleverly conceal will then begin oozing out.

If your husband is the one who hurt you, your well of resentment can be extremely deep. Those you love the most will always be the ones who hurt you the greatest. Why? You must love someone to be hurt by them. Where there is no love, frankly, you will not care. You may remain married. You may believe God is truly restoring. All the while, you may be deceiving yourself. It is possible you have not yet experienced forgiveness in its purest form.

How will you know if resentment is still controlling you?

Resentment will cause you to begin pulling away. You will stop looking for ways to please your husband. It will hide under the umbrella of forgiveness. Every now and then, resentment will peek out from wherever it was hiding, causing you to treat your husband differently. You won't think to bake his favorite cake. You won't get excited about shopping for a special surprise gift. Candlelight dinners, love notes, and all of the sweet little extras won't even cross your mind. If he asks something of you, you're likely to forget to take care of it. You will find yourself keeping your distance, staying busy and spending less time with him. You will no longer be interested in listening when he speaks. Looking directly into his eyes will become more difficult.

The respect, admiration and honor you once felt for him will begin to fade away. These changes will be subtle, and you will hardly realize they are happening.

My dad and I were very close. When he died suddenly at only sixty years old, I began to put up a wall without realizing what I was doing. I later learned our brains do this almost automatically. It's like a built-in defense system to avoid pain. I was my dad's princess and losing him hurt. He was still young, and I wasn't ready to let him go. I feared loving anyone after his death because I didn't think I could bear the pain of another loss of someone I loved so much. I found myself pulling away from everyone close to me, even my husband, and shutting them out of my life. I knew they could not understand my pain, so I would not allow their love to penetrate my wall. There was another problem with the wall I had built. My self-built wall also made it impossible for me to love others. The greater the hurt, the higher, wider and thicker the wall becomes, with less love being given or received.

If your spouse has hurt you, decide for yourself if you have built or are building a wall. Has your defense system gone into action? Are you afraid of letting him back into your heart? The fear of getting hurt again may have put a wedge in your marital relationship. It may have changed your ability to trust him or the way you demonstrate your love toward him. If you are dealing with a repeat offender, you may have built more than a wall. You may have built a huge fortress.

Jesus settled the issue with the number of times to forgive when he responded to Peter's question with the answer, "...*Until seventy times seven*" (Matt. 18:22). In other words, we should forgive as often as necessary. The power of the Holy Spirit will have to penetrate and destroy our walls or fortresses so we will be able to forgive.

As women, we might appear fragile, but we can be tough when we have to be. We hold grudges and accumulate ammunition for the next battle. When something happens, everything we have accumulated comes off the shelf. The battle is not over until the last bullet is shot.

Thankfully, the Lord's thoughts are not ours. Neither are His ways. His thoughts and ways are much higher than ours, as the heavens are higher than the earth (Isa. 55:8-9). Aren't you glad Jesus treats us better than we deserve to be treated? Jesus requires only two things from us, confession and repentance. If Jesus can forgive us, why can't we forgive our husbands? I ask you this question, "Have you forgiven?"

When you were saved, Jesus removed all of your condemnation and set you free from your guilt and shame. He said, *"Neither do I condemn thee; go, and sin no more"* (John 8:11). He gave you a fresh new start.

The next thing Jesus did was to cleanse you from all unrighteousness. All you had to do was confess your sins, and He was faithful and just to forgive you and cleanse you (1 John 1:9).

He purified you. He removed the filth of sin and made you pure. He said, *"Come now, and let us reason together; though your sins be as scarlet, they shall be as white as snow; though they be red like crimson, they shall be as wool,"* (Isa. 1:18).

Jesus sanctified you and separated you from your sin. He removed your sin as far as the east is from the west (Psa. 103:12). He removed your sins so far out of your life, it is as if you had never sinned.

Jesus justified you. Jesus blotted out your sins for His sake and chose not to remember them (Isa. 43:25). Unlike us, you will never hear Jesus say, *"Remember when."*

Jesus healed you. In His mercy, He healed your soul (Psa. 41:4).

What an example Jesus gives us of true forgiveness! Even in forgiveness, His life was a pattern for His children to follow.

It was His forgiveness that made you whole. It was His forgiveness that gave you a new start, a second chance.

> *"And the scribes and the Pharisees began to reason, saying, Who is this which speaketh blasphemies? Who can forgive sins, but God alone? But when Jesus perceived their thoughts, he answering said unto them, What reason ye in your hearts?"* [Jesus always knows our hearts.] *"Whether is easier, to say, Thy sins be forgiven thee; or to say, Rise up and walk?"(Luke 5:21-23).*

If you think about it, when Jesus forgave you, *"rise up and walk"* was exactly what He was telling you. He was saying, "be healed and go on your way." He did not want you to lay down in self-pity and hopelessness. He wanted you whole.

Jesus was merciful to our unrighteousness (Heb. 8:12). What if you were to see a poor man begging on the street? If he was hungry and cold, you would feel sorry for him. You might do a quick drive-by and pray for him as you passed. If so, you would have demonstrated sympathy. If God's mercy had been operating in your life, you would have stopped your car, given him some food to satisfy his hunger, or provided him with clothing to keep him warm. Your mercy would have alleviated his distress because mercy is not a passive activity. Mercy takes action.

<u>MERCY</u> – THE OUTWARD MANIFESTATION OF PITY, WITH PEACE BEING THE RESULTING EXPERIENCE IN THE HEART OF MAN.

Therefore, you have the power to give peace, one of the most precious gifts you can give to another individual.

If Jesus did all these things for you through forgiveness and you are now a child of God, how can you make excuses for your inability to forgive others? That's just it--you cannot. Jesus knew the importance of forgiveness when He laid out a conditional promise to you.

"For if ye forgive men their trespasses, your heavenly Father will also forgive you; But if ye forgive not men their trespasses, neither will your Father forgive your trespasses," (Matt. 6:14-15).

There were *three lessons* to be learned here:

1. If you forgive others, Jesus will forgive you.
2. If you refuse to forgive others, Jesus will not forgive you.
3. It is just as important to others that you forgive them, as it is to you that Jesus forgives you.

"Therefore is the kingdom of heaven likened unto a certain king, which would take account of his servants. And when he had begun to reckon, one was brought unto him, which owed him ten thousand talents. But forasmuch as he had not to pay, his lord commanded him to be sold, and his wife, and children, and all that he had, and payment to be made. The servant therefore fell down, and worshipped him, saying, Lord, have patience with me, and I will pay thee all. Then the lord of that servant was moved with compassion, and loosed him, and forgave him the debt. But the same servant went out, and found one of his fellow servants, which owed him an hundred pence; and he laid hands on him, saying, Pay me that thou owest. And his fellow servant fell down at his feet, and besought him, saying, Have patience with me, and I will pay thee all. And he would not; but went and cast him into prison, till he should pay the debt. So when his fellow servants saw what was done, they were very sorry, and came and

told unto their lord all that was done. Then his lord, after that he had called him, said unto him, O thou wicked servant, I forgave thee all that debt, because thou desiredst me; Shouldest not thou also have had compassion on thy fellow servant, even as I had pity on thee? And his lord was wroth, and delivered him to the tormentors, till he should pay all that was due unto him. So likewise shall my heavenly Father do also unto you, if ye from your hearts forgive not every one his brother their trespasses," (Matt. 18:23-35).

In this parable of the unmerciful servant, there is a servant who owed his king 10,000 talents. Scripture does not say whether the talents were gold or silver. Either way, the servant was indebted to the king for more money than he could possibly repay. In like manner, you may continue to work for the rest of your life, and it would still be impossible for you to repay the debt Jesus paid in full for you so freely at Calvary.

This king wanted justice which always demands satisfaction. Have you ever wanted satisfaction when you were wronged?

This king had no compassion. In an attempt to get justice, he commanded this man be sold, his wife, his children and all of his possessions. Every sin will be judged.

The enemy never operates out of a heart of compassion, and he never stops with the destruction of only one family member. The destruction of his wife, his children and his possessions followed. Don't be deceived. If there is sin in your life, your husband and children will sense it and suffer the effects of your sin. If there is sin in your husband's life, you and your children will sense it and suffer the effects of his sin. The devil will not stop until he has totally destroyed your whole family unit.

If your husband has hurt you, he may cry pools of tears, he may beg and plead for your forgiveness, and he may apologize over and over again. Isn't it true, though, there is absolutely nothing he can do or say that will remove the pain he has caused in your heart? However, there is something you can do. It is called forgiveness. You can give glory to God by forgiving your husband.

By following the example Jesus set, by being obedient to the Word of God, and by putting your faith in the Lord Jesus Christ, you can forgive. Through the power of forgiveness, you can be healed.

This king was finally moved with compassion at the servant's pleading, and he loosed him and forgave him his debt. When you forgive your husband, you are releasing him, unlocking the chains that have him bound and setting him free. The forgiveness of the debt is the loosing of the debtor. Allowing forgiveness to flow from you to your husband opens the channel of forgiveness from God into your own life as well.

This servant was forgiven and released from his debt, but notice he was not discharged from his duties. He went right back to work. I've heard this said by many, "I've forgiven my husband, but my marriage is over!" Why does it have to be over? When you forgive your husband, you will be releasing him from the penalty of his sin--not from his duties as a husband and a father. After all, even if he leaves the home, he will be your children's father until the day he dies. You need to make a choice to work on your marital relationship. Determine in your heart to forgive him as well as love, trust and respect him, as unto Christ.

Never fear forgiving someone, especially your husband. When Jesus forgave you, do you remember how much you loved Him? Would you have wanted to take Him for granted or walk all over Him? Not a chance! Don't believe the devil's lies. Your husband will not walk on you. Instead he will be grateful for your forgiveness and for your unconditional love. In fact, when the Lord opens your husband's eyes and the blinders are removed, his love for you will be magnified. You may fear he will sin again or hurt you again, and he might. Did you ever stumble or sin again after you were forgiven, or did you automatically become perfect? Allow the Lord to work in his life and trust and believe the Lord for your husband's soul to be preserved and for your marriage to be healed.

Un-forgiveness will cause a person's sins to be retained, binding them, immobilizing them and imprisoning them. An un-forgiven person will struggle with overcoming their failures for years. Un-forgiveness will cause a person to give up. Jesus did not die on the Cross for you to cause anyone, regardless of their sin, to give up. He wants them to get up. He wants them whole. Don't be guilty of wrapping a person in chains, fastening the lock and throwing away the key.

This servant, even after being forgiven for such a great debt, would not forgive a fellow servant for owing him only a hundred pence. He had his fellow servant put in prison, turned him over to the jailers, and showed him no compassion. He did not deliver the same treatment to his fellow servant he had received from his master. His fellow servants observed his behavior and reported him for his wickedness. [Isn't this just like the world? They are watching your life and noticing the way you treat others. Your life must be a living testimony of the love of Jesus.] The master was angry and had him brought to the jailers who would torment and torture him until his debt was fully paid.

Jesus makes the urgency of forgiveness very clear in the Book of Matthew, chapter 18, verses 34-35. If we want to be forgiven, we must forgive.

Un-forgiveness will bring torment in this life and throughout eternity. All you need to do to avoid this is to treat others with the same loving forgiveness you received from the Lord. Jesus forgave all your sins. He held back nothing. He expects no less from you. You must release those who have sinned against you. You must hold back nothing.

My husband and I have a preacher friend who publicly shared there had been occasions in his life where he had a difficult time forgiving a few individuals who viciously attacked him and his ministry. He teasingly said he had prayed, "Lord, I know your Word says that 'vengeance is mine, saith the Lord,' but oh Lord, please let me be your vessel." The truth is, at some point in your life, you may face a situation that seems impossible to forgive. You may wish you could be a vessel of vengeance. Vengeance will never be yours to take.

You might believe you tried everything within your power, and you cannot find it in your heart to forgive. You might believe you were too badly hurt. You might not verbally express it, but you feel the person does not deserve to be forgiven. If you are depending on your own strength and your own goodness, you are correct. You will wrestle and struggle to consider yourself as anything else but a victim. However, if you are a Christian filled with the love of God, all you have to do is allow the love of God to flow out of you. The Lord will forgive through you.

How many times have you asked the Lord in prayer, "Lord, will you help me to be a vessel of honor?" This is your opportunity. Be a vessel God can use. Allow His love, His compassion and His mercy to touch someone through you. Ask the Lord in prayer to break down every wall separating you from the one who hurt you.

Was this person your spouse? Ask the Lord to help you see your husband through His eyes of compassion. When you do, you will become more concerned with relieving your husband's pain and less concerned with your own. You are battling for your husband's soul. Time is short, and you cannot allow yourself to be controlled by selfishness, anger or bitterness.

> *"For we wrestle not against flesh and blood, but against principalities, against powers, against the rulers of the darkness of this world; against spiritual wickedness in high places. Wherefore take unto you the whole armour of God, that ye may be able to withstand in the evil day, and having done all to stand," (Eph. 6:12-13).*

Put on the full armor of God (Eph. 6:14-17), and keep your focus on Jesus. The more you clothe yourself with the character of Jesus, the more Jesus will be able to flow out of you to touch the lives of others. You will learn to love the way Jesus loves. It's that simple. We always think forgiveness is so complicated, but it's not.

The truth is that we are only the *conduit* of His forgiveness. It is not our own. His forgiveness flows through us. We have no power in ourselves to forgive sin.

Forgiveness is an extremely powerful force.

There is freedom in forgiveness. There is healing in forgiveness. There is life in forgiveness.

I ask you this question one last time, "Have you forgiven?"

CHAPTER SIXTEEN
DAD, HAS THE STORM ENDED?

Hundreds of men, women, boys and girls flood into a church building hungry to hear from the Lord. The worship is powerful, and the Lord's presence is evident. The minister steps up to the pulpit and shares God's message to the congregation. Days have been spent seeking the Lord in prayer and study, in preparation for the right message and for a move of God in the service. Some are saved, some are healed, and many are touched by the power of God. Being directed by the Holy Spirit and seeing the Lord move in such power is exhilarating. It is a mountaintop experience.

The service then ends. The battle for souls is over for the night, and the minister is mentally and physically exhausted. Have you ever seen someone preach under the anointing of

God, pray for a multitude at the altar, and become physically weakened by the end of the service? I have been in services where ministers, both men and women, had to be helped out of the sanctuary after the altar services. It is the end result of pouring out everything within them in order to minister effectively to others. The spirit is strong, but the flesh is weak.

Do you know it is in this weakened state, after victories were won for God's kingdom, the enemy will come to them? The devil will whisper the sermon delivery was poor; some part of the message upset Sister Jones; the sermon went right over everyone's head; the folks were not paying attention; the message was not clear; or someone else could have done a better job. After a night of battling for souls, the enemy will attack their tired minds and weakened bodies and attempt to make them feel like complete failures.

Why do you think the enemy comes whispering in your ear after a major spiritual victory in your life? It is because you are tired and weary from battle. It is then you are most vulnerable. Your guard is down, and you are caught unprepared.

Compare battling for souls to being in a hurricane. Have you ever been through a hurricane? [If you live in the New Orleans area, this would be an understatement.] If so, you will understand the amount of preparation prior to its arrival.

During Hurricane Betsy on September 9, 1965, the winds raged outside our home. We could hear roof shingles flying and loose items hitting the house. Everything that could be shaken was shaken with fierce winds gusting over 125 miles per hour. Within minutes, there was complete silence. As a thirteen year-old, I thought the storm was over. We stepped outside, and I can remember the hush of silence. The quiet seemed eerie and unnatural. Everything was calm. I looked up and asked, "Dad, has the storm ended?" My dad explained we were in the eye of the storm, and he hurriedly escorted me back inside for safety. Several minutes later, the storm began raging once more. Finally, the noise outside quieted down. I asked, "Now, has the storm ended?"

We went to sleep that night feeling relieved. The storm had ended. However, the very next morning, Dad yelled from outside that water was flowing down our street and rising fast. We had to evacuate immediately. In a flash, we grabbed a few precious items and fled. We may have been prepared for the storm's arrival, but we were not at all prepared for the days following the storm. We were away from our home for weeks, waiting for the water to recede so that we could return home to clean up the mess. Everyone, including me, forgot my birthday while living in survival mode. When we arrived home, the stench was nasty and there was so much work to do. Since the bayou had overflowed its banks, we had to watch for snakes and other critters.

On August 29, 2005, Hurricane Katrina left its devastating blow on the Mississippi Gulf Coast, the city of New Orleans, and surrounding parishes of Louisiana. Multitudes lost their homes. Houses and slabs were literally wiped off the face of the earth. No one living in those areas could have been prepared for life after the storm. Several years after Hurricane Katrina, I still had clients who would break down and cry at my office desk, representative of entire families who were still struggling to pull their lives back together.

As a wife, when you are trying your best to save your marriage, you are in a storm. The time for preparation should have been before the storm's arrival, not after you find yourself being tossed to and fro by the raging winds. Of course, there are those storms, like tornadoes, that hit with force, surprise and leave nothing in their paths but devastation. Regardless of how violent or sudden your storm, you are not fighting against flesh and blood. You are fighting against principalities, powers, rulers of darkness of this world and spiritual wickedness in high places. That's why you must be clothed in the full armor of God.

A troubled marriage is not an insignificant thunderstorm. Consider it a life-threatening Category 5 hurricane! You are battling for the souls of your husband and children. As you give of yourself to save your marriage and family, you will be emptying yourself and pouring out everything within you on a daily basis. Many times, you will feel you are giving more than you have to give. You will become weary and empty--physically, spiritually, emotionally and mentally--when you are giving all to save your marriage.

The Lord delights in those who give their best to minister to the needs of others. Therefore, He will delight in you as you give your best to save your marriage. Ministers cannot always see the demonic forces they are battling or the victories being won in the spiritual kingdom when they preach. Similarly, you will not always see the demonic forces you are fighting or the victories taking place in the spiritual realm as you fight for your marriage. You might miss the fact that God is working in your home and family in a mighty way.

You must re-fuel to survive. You will burn out quickly if you are leaning on your own strength. You must spend time with the Lord, in His Word and in prayer. Your fuel for the next day will depend on the time you spend with Him. Realize He is your lifeline, even more so in the heat of battle. Prepare yourself so you will not run short of the strength needed to get you through the work ahead.

The wrath of Hurricane Betsy passed over our city, never to return again. However, my family still had to face and overcome the remnants of the hurricane. Hurricane Katrina will never return, but it will take years for people to rebuild. Your storm will also pass. You too will have much work to do, as you face the aftermath of your storm.

Think about Elijah who had many mountaintop experiences. He had numerous victories in battle. He had slain all the prophets of Baal with a sword. He had clear direction and protection from the Lord, ravens brought him bread, and a widow woman provided for him miraculously. He even saw the Lord control the rain and give life back to a dead child. He saw all the people fall to their knees as the fire of the Lord fell and consumed the burnt sacrifices, the wood, the stones and the dust, and licked up the water that was in the trench. If anyone knew the power of God, Elijah knew God was able to do anything.

Basking in the victory of the Lord and with the hand of the Lord upon him, he ran twenty miles to Jezreel. It was there he learned Jezebel wanted his life. Wouldn't you think this man would be fearless, a mighty man of God? Not so. In fear, he ran eighty miles farther and hid himself away in a cave. Tired and weakened from battle, he was no match for her.

His fight was gone. His strength was gone. He pitifully prayed to the Lord to die. He was not prepared to face another enemy, especially one like Jezebel. Do you think the devil may have been whispering in Elijah's ear? I believe so.

You may get battle weary and feel you cannot go one more day, face one more setback. You may end up whining like Elijah or wanting to pull away, run or hide. The Lord did not forget Elijah, and He will not forget you. He knows your every thought, and He is aware of your every fear.

Victories are great and being an overcomer is wonderful. Be careful not to become complacent, though, after the storm has passed. Once all hurt has been forgiven, restoration has taken place, all has settled down, and a mighty victory has been won for God's kingdom, it is then you must beware. The enemy does not give up easily.

When you are enjoying the victory and rejoicing in the Lord's goodness, the enemy will come again to complete his task. The enemy will speak words of discouragement to you. He will try to create doubt in your mind and heart. He might whisper to you, "You should have divorced him." You might hear, "He doesn't love you." He may appeal to your pride and ask, "How could you be such a fool?" He may even say, "You would have been better off without him." The devil's ultimate goal is death, and as long as you give him an open ear, he will come in, and in New Orleans talk, he will "mow you down." He knows just what button to push to upset you or fill your heart with fear. Bring every thought captive to the obedience of Christ and do not entertain his lies (2 Cor. 10:4-5).

The Lord will keep you safe, and he will lead and guide you. Throughout your storm's fury, you will feel as if you are in the eye of the storm, safely protected and covered from the debris hurling around you. The Lord will also be with you after the storm, helping you to heal, giving you the strength and ability to make your marriage whole. He sent ministering angels to Elijah, and the Lord will minister to you. He promised:

> "...before they call, I will answer; and while they are yet speaking, I will hear," (Isa. 65:24).

Elijah was sensitive to hearing the Lord's voice. It is imperative we learn to hear His voice, too. In Elijah's case, he knew the Lord was not in the wind, He was not in the earthquake, and He was not in the fire. Elijah clearly recognized He was in the gentle stillness of a still, small voice. Will you recognize His voice when the Lord speaks to you?

"My sheep hear my voice, and I know them, and they follow me," (John 10:27).

No storm lasts forever. The winds of your storm may have been furious, instilling fear in your heart. They may have shaken you or terrified you. They may have left you with horrible memories or caused you seemingly irreparable damage.

Your home, symbolizing your marriage, may have only lost a few shingles, it may be flattened to the ground, or it may be completely out of sight. God knows how to restore and rebuild.

Regardless of the amount of damage to your marriage, God will meet your every need and heal your every hurt. He's able to repair and restore everything the devil has destroyed.

If repairs are not enough, He will completely rebuild your marriage from the foundation up. He is your provider. He will provide you with everything you need to start over again.

Look to the east! The sun shall rise again!

LORD, HEAL OUR MARRIAGE

CHAPTER SEVENTEEN
I CRIED TO THE LORD!

Regardless of how difficult your situation, I want you to learn the power of prayer.

Consider the story of Daniel and the lions' den. Daniel did not allow anything to interfere with his daily prayer life or his devotion to God. He was immovable. He found the time to pray regardless of where he was, who he was with, or what he was facing.

You may feel, like Daniel, you are facing a lions' den. You may be ridiculed for your faith, and you may feel your husband has become your greatest enemy. Nevertheless, when your ways please the Lord, He will make even your enemies to be at peace with you (Prov. 16:7).

Notice that while the Lord did not spare Daniel from experiencing the lions' den, He did deliver Him from the power of the lions.

> *"Then the king arose very early in the morning, and went in haste unto the den of lions. And when he came to the den, he cried with a lamentable voice unto Daniel; and the king spake and said to Daniel, O Daniel, servant of the living God, is thy God, whom thou servest continually, able to deliver thee from the lions? Then said Daniel unto the king, O king, live for ever. My God hath sent his angel, and hath shut the lions' mouths, that they have not hurt me; forasmuch as before him innocency was found in me; and also before thee, O king, have I done no hurt. Then was the king exceeding glad for him, and commanded that they should take Daniel up out of the den, So Daniel was taken up out of the den, and no manner of hurt was found upon him, because he believed in his God,"* (Dan. 6:19-23).

Why do you think Daniel had confidence in his God?

Daniel served God continually. He had a faithful prayer life. He knew the powerful God he worshipped. He knew he could trust the God he served. He had confidence he was innocent before God.

When Daniel was lifted out of the den of lions, it is interesting to note that not one wound was found on him. Daniel was not spared from the lions' den, but God sent an angel to protect him while in the lions' den.

In the same way, when Shadrach, Meshach and Abednego were thrown into the fiery furnace, they trusted their God was able to take care of them. They were not spared from the furnace experience, but they knew their God would be with them. They were committed to serve God, whether He delivered them from the furnace or not.

> *"Shadrach, Meshach, and Abednego, answered and said to the king, O Nebuchadnezzar, we are not careful to answer thee in this matter. If it be so, our God whom we serve is able to deliver us from the burning fiery furnace, and he will deliver us out of thine hand, O king. But if not, be it known unto thee, O king, that we will not serve thy gods, nor worship the golden image which thou hast set up,"* (Dan. 3:16-18).

> *"Then Nebuchadnezzar the king was astonished, and rose up in haste, and spake, and said unto his counselors, Did not we cast three men bound into the midst of the fire? They answered and said unto the king, True, O king. He answered and said, Lo, I see four men loose, walking in the midst of the fire, and they have no hurt; and the form of the fourth is like the Son of God,"* (Dan. 3:24-25).

Why do you think Shadrach, Meshach and Abednego had confidence in their God?

They believed in Him to the point they were willing to give up their lives if necessary. They refused to worship any other gods. They were committed. They walked around in the midst of a blazing furnace and they, too, were not hurt. Jesus Himself joined them in the furnace.

Do you realize Jesus walks with you regardless of what you are going through?

He is always with you--during good times and bad. Regardless of what the circumstances look like, you can put your trust and confidence in Jesus.

You may feel you are living in a lions' den or walking in a fiery furnace. The King of Kings is right by your side. He will bring you through your trouble and protect you from hurt. Life does not exempt you from trials. Thankfully, the Lord will walk with you through those difficult times.

> *"...Fear not: for I have redeemed thee, I have called thee by thy name; thou art mine. When thou passest through the waters, I will be with thee; and through the rivers, they shall not overflow thee: when thou walkest through the fire, thou shalt not be burned; neither shall the flame kindle upon thee,"* (Isa. 43:1-2).

Through prayer, the Lord will warn you, prepare you, strengthen you and direct you. It is through your prayers of faith that the Lord will hear your cries for help and respond.

In my personal prayer life, I have always had a habit of walking and praying. To be honest, moving keeps me from falling asleep while I am praying. When no one is home, I like to walk through my house from room to room and pray over our home and family. I still anoint my husband's pillow with oil and pray earnestly for God to bless him, keep him, protect him, and use him for His glory. I pray for my children and their families for God's purpose to be fulfilled in their lives and for their lives to bring glory to God.

Years ago, as I was making my rounds praying through our home, I felt the Lord's presence in a powerful way. A spirit of intercession came over me as I was praying for my husband.

> *"Likewise the Spirit also helpeth our infirmities: for we know not what we should pray for as we ought: but the Spirit itself maketh intercession for us with groanings which cannot be uttered. And he that searcheth the hearts knoweth what is in the mind of the Spirit, because he maketh intercession for the saints according to the will of God,"* (Rom. 8:26-27).

I felt such heaviness, like the weight of the world had been placed on my shoulders. My strength weakened, and I fell to my knees. I knew the Lord was showing me something was terribly wrong. I prayed until I finally felt a release. I knew when I finished praying that day, regardless of what I would go through, my battle had already been won in the Spirit. I knew I had definitely "prayed through," and the Lord heard me from His holy hill.

Later the same week, I had a dream that I knew was from God. In the dream, I saw a spider web, and it was extremely large. The web was woven tightly, and it was beautifully and intricately designed. In the center of the web was a man. As the spider worked diligently to wrap him and fasten him to the web more and more tightly, he would struggle and struggle to pull free, only for another part of his body to get caught in the web. The spider would then rush to the site to fasten that part of his body. It seemed it was impossible for him to free himself from this web. He was trapped and needed help. The man's strength was weakening, and he couldn't fight anymore. I watched as the spider drew closer. I knew it was going in for the kill, and I feared the man was going to die. In my dream, I remember trying to tell him to call on Jesus. I kept trying to get him to hear me, and I woke up yelling for him to call on Jesus.

In addition to that powerful time of prayer and the unusual dream, I had spent the past several months teaching the young married group during Sunday school. Surely, if there was something wrong with my marriage, I should have known it.

Unfortunately, I thought everything was fine, only to find out things were not as they seemed. Was I in the furnace alone? No. Was I in the lions' den alone? No. I had been teaching a marriage class only to find out my own marriage was falling apart. At the time, I felt like a complete failure as a wife and teacher. However, the Lord walked with me each and every day. I didn't have to walk alone. During this difficult time in my life, He carried me and made His presence real.

Let's turn this situation around and try to see it through God's eyes. Do you think it was mere coincidence I was asked to teach a marriage class? By teaching, I had made a concentrated effort to learn the Word of God as it applied to marriage. Now, I could rely on the Word of God that was in my heart. The Lord had prepared me in advance for my furnace experience.

Secondly, the Lord had revealed to me in prayer there was trouble on the horizon. I had time to pray and win the battle in the Spirit before the details were made known to me.

Finally, the Lord had warned me in the dream that my husband was in trouble and had fallen into a trap. He opened my eyes to the devil's snare. He showed me the enemy was busy working his web of destruction.

The Lord showed me my husband's need for help, gave me a heart of compassion, and gave me the assurance everything was going to be all right. All of this happened as a result of prayer.

Prayer will release the power of God to move in on the scene. Just as Daniel's prayers and trust in God brought about a miracle in his life, you can trust the Lord to perform a miracle in your life. In the same way Shadrach, Meshach, and Abednego were able to trust the Lord to deliver them through the fiery furnace, you can trust the Lord to be with you. Regardless of how vicious the lions or how hot the blaze, the Lord is able to bring you through your trouble to a brighter day.

"God is our refuge and strength, a very present help in trouble," (Psa. 46:1).

Be diligent in your prayer life.

In later years, I learned a powerful lesson about prayer from our pastor when he first came to our church. Many mornings, I would come into the church office, only to hear him down the hall in his office crying out to God on behalf of the families in our congregation. When problems would arise in the church, I observed his solutions were often different than mine would have been. He didn't react to circumstances nor did he handle things the quick-and-easy way. He was longsuffering and a pastor with great wisdom. His experience as a missionary on the foreign field had taught him how to trust God to fight his battles. He knew the importance of waiting on God and not getting ahead of Him. I noticed he did not take spiritual matters into his own hands. Instead, he took every situation to God in prayer, and He waited on God to move. I was amazed at how God's timing was always perfect. He told me one day the key was learning to recognize when God was moving and to move with Him. This pastor probably has no idea his prayer life ministered to me in such an invaluable and powerful way.

Please understand I would never begin to claim to know all there is to know about prayer nor would I ever claim to have a perfect prayer life. However, this one thing I do know. My times in prayer gave me the confidence that God heard me and the complete assurance He would meet me at my point of need. The confidence God was with me was what carried me through those desperate times.

"I cried unto the Lord with my voice, and he heard me out of his holy hill," (Psa. 3:4).

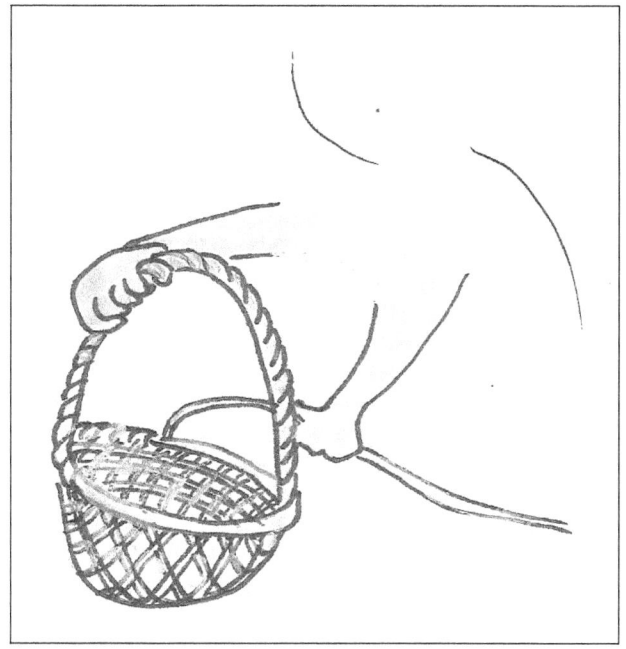

CHAPTER EIGHTEEN
A MASTER BASKET WEAVER!

I wrote this book and stored it in my closet years ago, thinking it was finished--until I had a dream this past year. In my dream, which I believe to be prophetic, I clearly heard a voice telling me to be a master basket weaver. All I could see in the dream were hands weaving a basket, but I could hear a deep voice teaching me.

Waking up, I jotted a few notes of what I could remember. What was God telling me? What could He mean? Why would He want me to be a master basket weaver? Is there such a thing? I strongly believed the voice of God was calling me to be a master basket weaver.

After doing a little online research, I discovered some amazing and interesting facts. Master basket weavers actually exist.

I found that in Africa alone there are approximately 2000 +/- Zulu women weaving baskets. A "Master Weaver" is recognized by the overall quality of the basket, especially in the tightness of the weave and the intricacy, as well as the size. Only master weavers can accomplish larger baskets and shapes. Only master weavers are capable of pulling consistently when making baskets, creating even baskets. In other words, they are experienced. They are skilled. Without skill and a very tight weave, baskets over three feet will collapse under their own weight. This consistency of high quality sets them apart from the rest. They are typically champions in their communities and villages, encouraging and training other weavers to excel and weave better quality baskets through their example. Out of the 2000 +/- weavers, only about 15 to 22 are consistent master weavers making the percentage very low.

Consistency of quality seems to be the most important factor when being considered a master weaver. More interestingly, the villages having a master weaver were the ones who produced weavers with consistent and excellent quality. They made a notable difference in their villages. In contrast, villages not having a master weaver present to teach them, ended up with weavers producing poor quality baskets.

What was God speaking to me through this dream?

I believe God was showing me master basket weavers are needed in our churches. In other words, experienced women, who trust God and walk by faith, are needed to teach younger women how to weave excellence into their families and homes. Many of today's homes have had no role models. The need is great. Many wives and mothers have not had the privilege of being taught by a godly mother. They do not understand how to love and minister to their families.

Building a good marriage and a solid family is much like striving to be a master basket weaver. I realized God was calling me to this task. Much of what He had already taught me through His Word needed to be shared with other women.

There are many similarities between striving to be a master basket weaver and striving to build excellence in our homes and families.

- Both require *strong foundations*.

    The foundation of each basket must be strong and tightly woven. Without a strong foundation, the basket will not hold together.

    Jesus Christ must be tightly woven into our families. Our strength comes from Him. We must have no other foundation but Him alone. He is the stone the builders rejected.

    "He only is my rock and my salvation; he is my defence; I shall not be greatly moved," (Psalms 62:2).

- Both require *time*.

    Master weavers devote hours per day to achieve excellence.

    A marriage of excellence will not happen overnight.

- Both require *dedication* and *self-discipline*.

    Master weavers discipline themselves to the task and are dedicated to see it through.

    Wives and moms must discipline themselves to the task. Excellence in their homes requires their total dedication.

- Both require *hard work.*

    The work of a master weaver is tedious and difficult.

    Being a wife and mom of excellence is very hard work. Most moms would agree that there is no job more demanding.

- Both require *commitment.*

    Master weavers are extremely committed to their villages. They recognize their villages depend on them.

    Wives and moms must stay committed through thick and thin and recognize their families are depending on them each and every day.

- Both are *labors of love.*

    Wives and moms, like master weavers, work hard and put forth untiring efforts to meet the needs of their families.

    "and worketh willingly with her hands," (Prov. 31:13).

    "She looketh well to the ways of her household, and eateth not the bread of idleness," (Prov. 31:28).

- Both require *patience.*

    Master weavers do not get weary in well doing.

    Patience is a key ingredient to being a good wife and mom. This fruit of the spirit will get you through the most trying days.

- Both require *vision.*

    Master weavers are very creative with colors, styles and patterns. They do not begin weaving a basket without first having a plan.

Weaving excellence into your home requires planning. It will not just happen!

- Both require a *willingness to correct mistakes.*

   Master weavers believe in excellence and do not settle for anything less.

   Do not settle for mediocrity. Your family deserves your very best. Be willing to learn ways to improve as a wife and mother.

- Both require a *willingness to start over.*

   Master weavers will, when necessary, unravel their mistakes and go back to the beginning rather than settle for mediocrity or poor quality.

   There are times it will be better to start fresh and approach the problem from another direction.

   When we first married and I tried to cook, I made many mistakes. I tried hard, but threw away several dishes that tasted horrible. The first time I attempted marshmallow fudge, it hardened in the platter like cement. When breaking it loose, it fell on the floor in one piece and bounced across the kitchen floor. My poodle sniffed it and ran away. The truth is cooking was very difficult for me, but I had to keep trying.

   Be willing to start over when necessary.

- Both require an *unwillingness to give up.*

   Master weavers are keenly aware others depend on them.

   Your husband and children depend on you. You can be a wife and mother of great value. Be steady. Press through. Don't give up. Be persistent.

- Both are used to *bless others.*

Master weavers bless their villages with their baskets, both in use and revenue.

In the same way, a godly home is a blessing to everyone it touches. The overflow extends far beyond your home address.

- Their baskets were *different in purpose.*

The purpose of each basket determined its style.

God has a divine plan and purpose for every individual, as well as for every family.

- Both require *consistency.*

Master weavers had to consistently produce high quality baskets. One every now and then did not qualify them to be called master weavers.

We must be consistent in weaving excellence into our homes. Putting forth extra effort only once in a while or on special occasions will never be enough.

- Master weavers *soak their reeds in water* to make them more pliable.

The ability of the reeds to bend makes them less likely to break and split.

We must be filled with the Spirit and yielded to the Spirit of God so that God can have His way in our lives.

- Both must be *tightly woven* to hold up under the pressures of life.

These tightly woven baskets are stronger, can carry more weight, and are more valuable.

Families who stay tightly woven to Jesus are stronger and can withstand the pressures of life.

These overcomers can be greatly used in the work of God's kingdom.

"And if one prevail against him, two shall withstand him; and a threefold cord is not quickly broken," (Eccl. 4:12).

- The high standards of excellence set by master basket weavers are *passed on to the next generation,* through their training and example of excellence.

In the same way, through the training of the older women, a high standard of excellence can be passed down from generation to generation. The younger wives and mothers can learn how to weave excellence in their homes and families.

"The aged women likewise, that they be in behaviour as becometh holiness, not false accusers, not given to much wine, teachers of good things; That they may teach young women to be sober, to love their husbands, to love their children," (Titus 2:3-4).

It is my prayer you take hold of the principles from God's Word outlined in this book, apply them to your personal lives, and then pass them on to your children, your grandchildren and others in your circle of influence. You must pray. Pray your lives become instruments of His mighty power. Pray your testimonies inspire others to believe and trust in Almighty God. Pray your lives glorify God.

We know Jesus is the Word (John 1:1), and He reveals Himself to us through His Word. The more you surrender your will to Him and apply the Word of God to your daily lives in obedience, the more others will recognize Jesus living in you.

Are you settling for mediocrity or setting high standards for your families? Are you striving to weave excellence in your homes? Do your actions consistently line up with God's Word? Most of all, are you setting a godly example for your children and grandchildren to follow? What are you passing on to the next generation?

Let's teach our loved ones, by example, the difference Jesus makes in our lives, our marriages and our homes. There is always room for improvement in each of our lives. Jesus has not stopped working on me, and He will continue to work on me until I meet Him on the streets of glory. How about you? Let's allow Jesus to transform us from glory to glory as He works in our lives, gently nudging us along to become the women of God He desires us to be.

It is my prayer this book has stirred your hearts and inspired you to give God your very best. Will you strive to weave excellence in your homes? As for me, I strongly desire to fulfill His call to be a master weaver. It is my prayer you will join me in this spiritual pursuit.

Allow the Lord to have first place in your lives; and, invite the Holy Spirit to be your teacher and your guide. Jesus is more than able to complete the good work He has begun in your lives, your marriages and your families.

Become weavers of excellence in your homes!

EPILOGUE
FROM THE HEART OF HER KING!
By John H. Youngblood, Jr.

I have encouraged Pam to publish this book for years, and I have read it from beginning to end more than once. In my opinion, it will be a tremendous blessing to many women. I am convinced it will be of great value to any wife willing to petition God for a better marriage. You have just learned many principles from the Word of God. With your trust firmly planted in Jesus Christ, I can assure you that you will reap great rewards as you apply those principles to your personal lives and marriages.

Most couples enter marriage with pre-conceived ideas, often expecting the ideal. Unfortunately, we end up with the real. In our marriage, neither of us was perfect. Both of us had many lessons to learn, and we made mistakes along the way as we strived to build a life together. In fact, Pam revealed many of her mistakes to you in the pages you have just read. She took it easy on me, allowing me the opportunity to write my own story one day.

Nevertheless, the main problem in our marriage was a sin problem. I take total responsibility for the heartache and recurrent hurt in our marriage. My life and family has been healed and abundantly blessed by the Lord. Having a wife who dared to believe God made this healing possible. She put her faith and trust in God when circumstances continued to weaken her faith. She made a choice to love and forgive me, a choice solely based on her personal conviction to obey God's Word.

Greatly misled and deceived, I believed I could please God, my wife and my family while I was home with them, and live a different life when I was away from them. I wasn't hurting anyone, I reasoned. After all, no one would ever know. As a young man, my job took me out of town frequently, allowing me many opportunities to make poor choices. I felt my family could not be hurt by my actions. I was living a lie. I was living a form of religion, going through the motions, and having no true personal relationship with Jesus Christ. I had convinced myself, though, I was serving the Lord. I was going to church, paying tithes, involved in church activities, and serving in various roles in the church. The whole time, my heart was far from being totally surrendered to Jesus Christ.

I was walking on very dangerous ground. The danger was that I actually saw myself as a Christian. I looked around at other men in the church, and with a carnal mind and a quick comparison, I felt I measured up as a good man and a good husband. I worked hard and took excellent care of my family. My family was not lacking for anything. I had attended church all my life, and I had served as an altar boy at a young age. I said grace before each meal. I even prayed with my young children at night before putting them to bed. I often did good works for others. I saw myself as sacrificing for my family as well as for others. I thought I measured up and was doing a pretty good job as a husband and father. Unfortunately, I was failing miserably in my Christian walk.

My wife forgave me many times for my ungodly choices. There is no doubt she forgave me many more times than I deserved. She continued to pray for me through our struggles. Most of all, she continued to love me. The more she prayed, the more my life became increasingly difficult. I asked the Lord to forgive me numerous times. I couldn't be happy regardless of what I did or where I went because I knew the real me. I would repent and then end up making poor choices again. Make no mistake--the devil was wreaking havoc in my life. I gave him an open door, and He was moving in for the kill. As God's Word tells us, the devil comes to steal, kill and destroy. What easier way for the enemy to attack a family unit than through the doors left open by its leader?

One day, I began telling my wife about a man we both knew who was living his life on the edge. He was walking the fence. She spun around, pointed at me and blurted out, "Thou art the man!" I could see the shock and surprise on her face. She had no idea at that moment where those words came from or why she said them to me. I knew. The Holy Spirit had put those words in her mouth as a warning. Unfortunately, I did not heed that warning.

While out of town on business a few months later, I went to a well-known nightclub with co-workers. I was talked into riding the mechanical bull. Pictures of me riding the bull eventually arrived at my house from co-workers, and my wife opened the mail. Since I was a man who pretended not to drink or frequent clubs or bars, can you imagine her surprise as well as her disappointment in me as she looked at those pictures? The fact is the Lord began exposing my secret sins.

The men who had most influenced my life had taught me by word and example that, "what your wife did not know could not hurt her." Of course, this is not true. Somehow, my wife always seemed to find out. Eventually, I did hurt her. The season of deceitfulness grew from days, to months, into years. Only God could have given Pam the strength and courage to hang in there. I would ask for forgiveness from her and from the Lord. We would try to begin again as if nothing had ever happened. I had great intentions and a desire in my heart to be the man of God I needed to be. Unfortunately, I always held part of me back and never truly surrendered to Him 100 percent, especially when it came to alcohol. This gave the devil an invitation and a wide entrance into my life.

One day, my wife finally had enough. In prayer, she told God she could not read my heart, but He knew my heart. She also knew I would never be able to fool Him. She told Him she couldn't be with me all the time, but He could. She was no longer praying for my protection or for my health. Her only concern was the condition of my soul. Therefore, she was putting her complete trust in Him to do whatever was necessary to set me free.

Can you guess what followed? That's right--trouble. I started having trouble in every area of my life. Nothing seemed to go my way. Things went from bad to worse, and I feared I had really crossed the final line. I had covered up my sinful life for a long time. How could she ever forgive me? Satan was telling me I couldn't live for God and I should move on, have fun and enjoy my life. Satan was telling me my marriage was over, my wife would never forgive me, and any future with her would be "hell on earth." My mind was filled with confusion. My life was a mess.

Through circumstances totally out of my control, the Lord saw fit to expose everything I had ever done in secret. At the time, I felt He was doing this to destroy me. He wasn't. He wanted me set free from sin, and He wanted our marriage to be made whole. The miracle was my wife was willing to walk through this painful time by my side. She still loved me in spite of my failures. She seemed to have a supernatural ability to see past my present condition and see a great future with me as a man of God.

I am sure there will be many ladies reading this book who have been hurt by men one or more times throughout their lives. I can make no excuses for these men who have broken your trust or wounded your spirits. Please, let me apologize and ask for your forgiveness on behalf of these men, so that you can be made whole. Be set free. Be healed, in Jesus' name!

Please remember this one main point. Hold onto Jesus like a bulldog holding onto a bone. Do not give up. Even when your husband seems unlovable, ask the Lord to help you show him love. It is God's love flowing through you that will pierce his hard heart and cause him to reach out to Jesus.

When I look back at my past, I have many regrets. There were many times I came close to death in car accidents, fights, or just being in the wrong place at the wrong time. The Lord would have been more than justified to lift His hand of protection from me. I am truly a living miracle of God's grace and mercy.

My wife wanted a better marriage, so she continued to pray and allow the Lord to change her. Godliness began developing in her life, and she grew into a more godly woman right before my eyes. The more she changed, the more obvious it became I was a phony. I was not what God wanted me to be. Sin had a strong hold on me. I was no longer able to justify my sinful condition by blaming my wife because she had lined her life up with God. I had to face myself for who I was, and I didn't like myself. In fact, I hated and was ashamed of who I had become. I had let God down, I had let my family down, and I had even let myself down. I did not want to be this person. It became clear to me I either had to repent once and for all or I would be playing with death--my death. God's Word tells us the wages of sin is death. I was really afraid God would not forgive me. The battle that was going on in my mind finally ended with my true repentance. Thankfully, the Lord was waiting with open arms, and He cleansed me of all unrighteousness. Today, He is continuing to mold me into the man of God He desires me to be.

Time was a good friend as God worked with us to heal and restore our marriage. Submitting to a higher purpose brought victory to our lives. Of course, there were consequences, but God helped us overcome. God was able to do the impossible in our lives. He never left us helpless or hopeless. His life-changing power positively transformed our lives and our marriage. I thank the Lord each day for His mercy and unconditional love.

Because of Jesus, we were saved, our marriage was healed, and our children were raised in a Christian home. I have been given an undeserved opportunity to pass on a godly heritage to our children and grandchildren. What a blessing. What a miracle. My family means everything to me. God has done so much for us and for our family. I cannot thank Him enough, and He gets all of the glory!

Trust Jesus with your marriage. He loves you and He loves your husband. In this last hour, don't give up. Jesus hears the cries of your heart. Your love and prayers could mean the difference in where your husband spends eternity.

Every time I watch the news, the soon coming of our King of Kings and Lord of Lords becomes more evident. With the increase of disease, earthquakes, floods, tsunamis, tornadoes, sink holes, the escalation of wars and rumors of wars, the deterioration of today's society, the increase of evil in our land, one truth becomes increasingly clear.

It will not be long before King Jesus splits the eastern sky and comes to take His children home.

> *"For the Son of man shall come in the glory of his Father with his angels; and then he shall reward every man according to his works. Verily I say unto you, There be some standing here, which shall not taste of death, till they see the Son of man coming in his kingdom,"* (Matt. 16:27-28).

Jesus is coming soon!
Let's be ready!

Pam can be contacted via e-mail: pdy907@yahoo.com.

All comments, feedback or praise reports on *Lord, Heal Our Marriage* are welcome. Pam and John are available for men's or women's ministry events and marriage seminars.

www.ingramcontent.com/pod-product-compliance
Lightning Source LLC
Chambersburg PA
CBHW060512100426
42743CB00009B/1290